Raising Confident Girls

100 Tips for Parents and Teachers

Elizabeth Hartley-Brewer

DEDICATION

For Georgia and her life-long friends Miranda, Avani, Lizzie and Jessica, with whom she has shared so much for so long

First published in the United Kingdom in 2000 by Vermilion, an imprint of Ebury Press

 Printed in the United States of America.

Cataloging-in-Publication data for this book is available from the Library of Congress.

ISBN 1-55561-321-7

Fisher Books is a member of the Perseus Books Group.

Find us on the World Wide Web at http://www.fisherbooks.com

Fisher Books' titles are available at special discounts for bulk purchases in the U.S. by corporations, institutions, and other organizations. For more information, please contact the Special Markets Department at the Perseus Books Group, 11 Cambridge Center, Cambridge, MA 02142, or call (617) 252-5298.

First printing, March 2001

1 2 3 4 5 6 7 8 9 10

Contents

Acknowledgments

The idea for this book and its partner, *Raising Confident Boys*, came from my editor, Jacqueline Burns. Had she not been such fun to work with, I may not have gone ahead with it. So I'd like to thank her, and Amy Corzine, who took over the reins during Jacqueline's maternity leave.

I am indebted to two teacher friends in particular, Dexter Hutt, Principal of Ninestiles School, and Gary Wilson, Head of English at Newsome High, who both gave precious time to long conversations and manuscript reading, which I needed and really appreciate. I would also like to thank Geoff Evans, of the C'mon Everybody project; Adrienne Katz, of the research organization Young Voice, which published *The Can-Do Girls*; Jo Adams, for her report *GirlPower*; and Alex Vear, a good, wise friend and mother of two daughters in the thick of growing up, for helping in various ways.

Finally, I'd like to thank my daughter, Georgia, who is just entering adolescence, for her constant support, love, and understanding. I wish her well for the adventure ahead.

CHAPTER 1

Understanding Her Challenges and Opportunities

Everything seems to be going right for girls. Their confidence, exam results and career opportunities are rising. Released from the prison of domestic life, they have a freedom that was unheard of fifty years ago. Many boys feel that girls have it easy and resent it, for the have-it-all world that beckoned their mothers seems like a go-and-get-it-all world to their daughters, and leaves boys behind.

Competent, successful superwomen have bred competent, successful supergirls—or have they? Not far under the surface of "girl power" lie new pressures and insecurities that come with our daughters' enhanced potential for success. Some, such as eating disorders, have arrived in the slipstream of that success. Others exist where success is absent, for success has certainly not come to all girls, who today manage a triple dose of expectation: to be academically and economically successful; to be emotionally independent and to achieve the heightened standard of beauty that cosmetics, clothes and even surgery can now provide. They are expected to look good for themselves and their female friends, not necessarily for the opposite sex, who are regarded as creating more problems than they are worth, hence the new female goal of emotional as well as economic independence. Alongside this emotional aloofness is an equally pervasive pressure for girls to be not only sexually aware but also sexually skillful. The magazines tell them how. It is an emotional minefield in which many vulnerable girls get blown up, as teenage pregnancy figures testify.

There are academic casualties, too. While many girls work the educational system to their advantage, some succeed only at considerable cost to their mental health and well-being. Others fail to make it at all. Two to three girls in every one hundred will attempt suicide at some time in their teenage years. Indeed, females between fifteen and nineteen are the highest single risk group for attempted suicide.

Some parents add to the pressures their daughters feel. Like them, they fall prey to the look-good, feel-good, get-rich-quick society. Mothers can look more stunning than their ugly duckling daughters for years, and they must be self-assured enough not to play this game.

The brighter side of the story is that at the beginning of the twenty-first century, females have more opportunities and are less restricted by their gender than ever before. There are few areas of sport, leisure or work that remain the exclusive preserve of males, in theory at least. Girls can have all this and also become mothers.

With so much available to girls, parents and teachers have the task of helping them make the most of their abilities. However, to maximize their chances and to protect themselves against the potential problems of their new position in society, girls need plenty of positive self-esteem and large doses of genuine self-assurance.

Girls must fashion a new femininity—one that will encourage integrity, respect for others and themselves, independence and autonomy while acknowledging their biological inclination to nurture. Femininity used to imply making oneself look pretty for men, being self-effacing, submissive, compliant and placid, always thinking of and caring for someone else's needs before addressing one's own. This is now rejected by most young women, but, in pushing themselves forward, some have simply imitated men.

A respectful regard for themselves *as female* is vital if they are to remain psychologically intact in the face of the abuse that so many suffer. They should not consider themselves weak or inferior to boys because they may be more emotional or don't always feel in control. Girls must acknowledge their own needs while recognizing other people's, see themselves as having worthwhile views and accept that they deserve care and respect from others.

The self-criticism, low self-esteem and dissatisfaction with their looks and performance that exist unexpressed behind even confident exteriors should be a matter of considerable concern. Girls thrive when people notice when they've done something well, listen to and take them seriously, and acknowledge their rights.

If girls are to become more self-assured, parents and other involved adults cannot start too soon. Building self-knowledge, identity, confidence and self-esteem—the constituents of inner strength—is the way to create a resilient young woman who is able to cope with challenges and an uncertain future with confidence.

CHAPTER 2

Meeting Her Needs

Girls' fundamental needs are the same as boys'. No one has an awareness of their gender until about the age of two, and most of us go on needing the same kind of essential support and care from those close to us throughout our adult lives. In addition to being fed and clothed appropriately and kept clean and healthy, young girls, like boys, also need emotional sustenance. They need to be loved and cherished, appreciated and valued, noticed, enjoyed and admired.

Girls thrive when these needs are met because they feel important and significant. When they feel secure and capable, when they are listened to, especially as a source of authority in relation to themselves, and when they are able to develop their talents, they grow up feeling strong inside and able to walk tall. By contrast, if a girl's basic needs are not met, she will feel neglected, separate, unworthy of attention and full of shame. Growing girls have special needs on top of these basic ones that relate to their future role in society. Parents and teachers should attend to these as well. Girls now require the confidence and flexibility to balance the demands of work and family and, at the same time, to manage the uncertainty of likely home and job changes. They should grow up able to love and trust without making themselves vulnerable to exploitation and abuse. Girls should be helped to become strong enough inside to defend themselves against any assault or intrusion on their physical and mental integrity, at home or at work.

During childhood, girls typically develop closer relationships with their mothers. When mothers are reluctant to let go, the possessiveness and competition that arise may make separation that much harder and more painful. It is not uncommon for intimacy to be associated with exploitation and emotional aggression. Intimacy should not be allowed to develop into dependency or domination.

Meeting our daughters' need for intimacy, support, honor and autonomy takes time and considerable effort. But if we don't put in that effort, we are likely to have to work much harder later on picking up the pieces of their consequent emotional distress.

1 Help her to believe in herself

As I left the house for my first date, my father told me that I looked wonderful and the boy was very lucky to be going out with someone so special. If he didn't appreciate that, he was the loser. He made me feel the best and gave me the strength to cope with anything.

If a girl has good self-esteem, she will automatically believe in herself as a capable and lovable person. She will have a clear and positive sense of who she is and will see herself in a favorable light. Girls with self-belief will be optimistic about what they can manage and achieve. They will be able to raise their sights, stand up for themselves and explore their potential. People who lack belief in themselves are filled with a generalized self-doubt that can make them feel guilty, shameful and inadequate.

No girl will believe in herself if someone has not first demonstrated belief in her competence and capability and considered her worthy of love, support and attention.

Parents

- Show faith and trust in your daughter—in her ability to decide certain things, to succeed at tasks, to manage her own personal care and to be responsible when she's old enough.
- Show her that you love and enjoy her in ways that will convince her.
- Beware of thinking, "I didn't get or need support, so she'll be the same." She is different. Also, people who "don't get" often turn this into "don't need" to cover up their own disappointment.
- Show love physically in ways other than kisses and hugs: For example, sit close to look at books, magazines or television, or on her bed at bedtime.

Teachers

- Teachers will not feel parental love for the girls in their class. However, they can make it clear that they enjoy, approve of and accept their students for who they are.
- Identify two or three girls in your class who show signs of low self-esteem. Try to talk regularly to each one and comment favorably on her various attributes and abilities.
- Giving special tasks to these girls can make them feel significant, noticed, reliable and trustworthy.

2 Show that you understand her

My six-year-old came home from school one day particularly irritable and tired. It turned out she'd had a difficult day bickering with her two best friends. She felt really low, but when I told her about "Two's company, three's a crowd" and explained the problems and dynamics of threesomes, even for adults, she brightened.

All children are frustrated when they're misunderstood. At first, they'll just be irritated, but when the mistake persists, they will begin to doubt themselves and their sense of reality. If your daughter's wishes, thoughts or experiences are continuously ignored or misinterpreted, it won't be surprising if she becomes resentful and angry.

You can show that you understand her by anticipating her needs and expressing her likely thoughts—though carefully—using phrases such as, "I guess you're feeling left out, am I right?" Posing the question at the end gives her room to disagree and keeps you from coming across as infuriatingly all-knowing—and possibly wrong.

Parents

- Accept the way your daughter sees the world—she does not have to agree with you, nor you with her.
- Value her uniqueness. Tell her what you admire and treasure about her.
- Look beyond her behavior at possible causes and feelings.
- Repeat what she says to you to make sure you've understood correctly: "So you want me to stay in tonight because you're fed up with me working late so much this week, right?"
- Remember her likes and dislikes.
- State what she's likely to feel: "You won't want to hear this, but I can't afford a new jacket for you this month."

Teachers

- Make a conscious effort to see patterns in a girl's work that might show you what makes her tick.
- Encourage classwork that draws on students' likes and dislikes. Try to remember a few of them for each student.
- For girls who seem particularly trying, list four reasons why this might be so, excluding "difficult personality."
- Use reflective listening phrases: "What I hear you saying is that you did not feel you knew enough to start this homework. Let's start from what you're sure you do know."

3 Approve of who she is, even if you dislike what she does

Every girl needs to be accepted and approved of for who she is, not just because she has been "good," "helpful" or "successful" and lived up to your ideal of who she should be. If she constantly fills a mold set by you, she'll lose her identity and have trouble feeling happy about who she is.

Young children are always getting into mischief because they are learning about rules, how things work and how to handle themselves. Clumsy reprimands convey disapproval and can do a lot of damage. If you want to comment on something your daughter has done, be clear that it's her actions you disapprove of, not her. This will leave her self-worth intact while she learns to manage her behavior and appreciate what flows from it.

Don't lose faith in her just because you are unhappy about a particular act or attitude. Don't leave her feeling devastated by your criticism.

Parents

- Think about your daughter's good points before you criticize a particular behavior, to help you think positively and make your comment specific.
- Avoid using the words "good" or "bad" about her behavior, because she'll take them as reflections of herself. Instead, talk about what it is she does that you like or dislike.
- Limit your disapproval to the moment by saying, "Right now, I find you . . ."
- Striking her with your hand or an object will do untold damage, including encouraging her to feel that you dislike her. She may then decide she is not good enough to be liked.

Teachers

- Identify something you like about each student. Then it is easier to state honestly that it's behavior that's the problem, not the girl herself.
- Describe in detail the behavior that is outside the rules. Avoid "You" statements: "I'm irritated by the way you are tapping your ruler" is less personally offensive and provocative than "You are being really irritating!"

4 Give plenty of praise

Children love to be noticed and to give pleasure. It is wonderful to see our daughters beam with pride when they have done something well and they know we have noticed. This is the essence of constructive praise.

Girls enjoy praise because they like to know that someone appreciates the effort they have made when they have tried. Praise also helps to develop self-discipline. Through praise and encouragement, girls receive clear, positive messages about how they should lead their lives—what it is they should do, instead of what it is they should *not* be doing.

Many people find it hard to be generous with praise. Being critical makes them feel in charge and all-knowing. Praise, on the other hand, can make them believe they've lost that powerful edge. Some don't know what to praise or what words to use. Others believe that praise will make a girl big-headed or lazy and over-satisfied with work that isn't perfect. But being noticed and appreciated usually makes girls try harder, and it shows them how to give positive feedback to others.

Parents

- Say things like "That's great!", "Fantastic!", "Good job!" and "Thanks, that was really helpful."
- Find something to notice and praise at least once every day.
- Girls can be praised for their thinking skills (their choices, ideas, problem solving), social skills (helpfulness, understanding, sharing, and flexibility), physical skills (running, tree-climbing, making things, sports) as well as for pleasing reports and grades.
- Be specific: Praise what she has done. Don't talk in general about how wonderful and smart she is.
- Able girls also need their effort recognized by their parents, even if they usually do well.

Teachers

- Encourage girls to evaluate and praise each other's work, so that praise doesn't always come from someone in authority.
- Help students to feel satisfied: "I bet you felt really happy with this when you finished it."
- Find something to praise every day, and include humor, sociability and creativity.
- If a girl rejects all praise, showering her with it won't work. Select one thing you find truly pleasing and repeat it three times every day for three weeks, so that she begins to believe and trust that it is true.
- Don't overdo it: Public recognition of success may lead to perfectionism and praise-dependency.

5 Spend time with her

I know my dad loves me, but I barely know him. I know he works hard to support us, but we hardly ever talk. It makes me feel as if I'm incomplete.

Research shows that children like to have their parents around, even if they're not actively doing anything with them. Girls like to see fathers as much as mothers. Even teenagers report wanting to see more of their parents, even if it is a case of being "seen but not heard."

Men and women work longer hours than ever before. This means they spend less time at home with their families. Girls cannot feel loved and lovable, believed in and believable, respected and respectable, if the people on whom they depend seem not to care. Only if the important adults in a girl's life give her time and attention can she feel validated and develop any kind of self-worth. Meeting your daughter's need for stress-free time with you, when you give her your undivided attention, will help her feel confident and significant.

Parents

• Presents are no substitute for presence: Don't try to buy your way out of being available.

• Spend time finding out what your daughter thinks and talking about what she has been doing.

• Play with her, watch her doing (or join in) her favorite activity or say, "Please talk to me while I wash the car," or "peel the vegetables" and so on.

• Keep every promise to visit, and stay in regular touch.

• Quiet time together can be as valuable as action-packed time.

• Try to do any office work you need to do at home in family space so that you're available.

Teachers

• Don't let bad behavior or learned helplessness (to which girls are particularly prone) be the only way to get your attention.

• If a student wants a conversation at an inconvenient moment, suggest another time when you can really listen to her.

• Each week, identify the withdrawn girls and organize with colleagues to make a special effort to speak to and engage with each one every day.

6 Communicate with touch and words

Touch often conveys what you want to say better than words do. It is far less open to misinterpretation and only takes a second. The positive touch is, for example, a full embrace or an arm around your daughter's shoulders. It can ask for nothing in return or seek a simple sign from her that she feels the same way. It can show her and others that she belongs to you. It can heal an argument and say you're sorry. It can console her after a disappointment, demonstrate your pride or be a show of equality and partnership.

Touch can reassure as well as relax, but it can also hurt. Hitting even a young girl will usually hurt her deeply, and simply pushing your daughter away when you're angry can be a signal interpreted by her as deep rejection. A girl who is never touched can feel ignored and ashamed of herself, and may become easy prey to inappropriate attentions from others.

Parents

- Little strokes of your daughter's forehead or hands at bedtime or while watching TV—or just sitting close—can be a way to get the habit of touch back into your family if it has disappeared.
- Experiment with using touch as an alternative to words.
- Some children don't like too much hugging. Don't force it. Just find other ways to get close, experience togetherness and show your love.

Teachers

- Child protection issues make many teachers reluctant to touch children. In any case, as girls grow older, it becomes increasingly difficult and inappropriate to do so. Just standing close to a student as you look over her work can show you accept her and feel no discomfort in her presence.
- Some teachers greet their class of young children individually as they enter the classroom, inviting each pupil to choose how to say hello each time—with a smile, a handshake or nothing at all if that's how they feel that day.

7 Respect her right to know

Most children thrive when they feel secure and can predict what will happen to them. The unexpected can be very unsettling. Sometimes things happen out of the blue and adults involved are equally surprised. But more often the adults know in advance and simply fail to keep a child informed.

Children need to be able to make sense of their world. If they can't, they live in social and emotional chaos. They make sense of life both through the patterns that emerge when life is ordered (when each day has a predictable shape to it) and through explanations when changes occur. Young children's brains develop by constructing meaningful patterns, so every child needs to make sense of knowledge and events before she can learn.

When you explain things to your daughter, you show that you respect her right to know, empathize with her need to make sense of her world, respect her ability to understand and trust her with the information.

Parents

- Try to tell your daughter about events before they happen and as they happen. Explain afterward why something happened.
- Tell her about your feelings and discuss hers.
- Talk to her about variations in routines and when partners and relationships change. Explain any absences.
- Inform her about decisions and the reasons for them.
- Give her the facts. Answer honestly her questions about such things as death and divorce, in terms she can comfortably understand.

Teachers

- Give students fair warning of any changes in classroom routines.
- If you know that you're going to be away, give them notice, and let them know who will take your place.
- Explain why any punishment or consequence is being imposed.
- Explain why a piece of work is either good or falls short of the required standard.
- Keep girls informed about the time it will take to grade important tests or projects, and explain any delay in returning work.

8 Constantly reinforce her sense of self-worth

Girls are like sand castles. One minute they stand perfect, proud, intact, seemingly impregnable against the enemy; the next, the tidal waters of self-doubt are lapping away at their foundations, causing a progressive collapse. We can't hold back the tide, but we can be on hand to dig furiously to reinforce our daughter's self-worth, so that when the tide recedes, there is something left. If we have enough knowledge and foresight, we can help her to establish herself above the tide line, but it's rare that we can spot safe territory in advance. There are no rocklike certainties in the world in which our girls live today.

The waves that erode a girl's foundations are fads and crazes, body image and fashion, pressure to be an academic or social success, and sexual activity. Just when she needs more than ever to be sure of herself, given the demands and uncertainties within her life, these forces try to flatten her into relentless uniformity. The more she loses her true self, the more she has to rely on image and peer approval to feel comfortable.

Parents

• Try not to let your daughter become obsessed with collectibles and fads. Help her remain her own person.

• Never refer, either approvingly or disapprovingly, to her weight or body shape, unless it is to counter her own negative comments.

• Always balance any comments about appearance by saying that it's what's inside that counts.

• If she says, "I won't be popular unless I . . ." (follow some trend or other), it's a sign that she's feeling insecure. Giving in will make her more dependent on conformity. Suggest reasons she can give to friends for not conforming, so she can resist them with more confidence.

Teachers

• Be vigilant to spot any signs of low self-worth in students. Step in with positive comments and approval if you hear them say anything self-deprecating.

• Encourage class discussions about any craze as it emerges, and stress constantly the importance of making up their own minds about what they like, want and need.

• If a girl says she is no good, stupid or knows nothing, challenge it, not with an outright denial, but by saying how you see her work: "I think your work is full of good ideas," or "I would not have been able to give that essay a B if you had known nothing."

9 Be her last refuge

When your daughter has been going through a tough time, when she has had enough and has no energy left to keep up a front, she'll need somewhere to hide, somewhere, and someone, to be her last refuge. This is the place where she can be herself, where—for a short time anyway—no one will hold her accountable and she is accepted unconditionally. Here she can truly relax, safe in the knowledge that someone is there for her, someone who will share her burdens for a while and give her some relief.

Home, for children, is the obvious place, and parents are the obvious people, because they matter. There may be times and situations, however, when parents feel they don't have the emotional reserves to give the consolation required. You might consider whether your daughter really needs anything except to be close to you, without saying or doing anything else. It might not take much to help her renew her faith in herself.

Parents

- If your daughter asks for forgiveness, accept her olive branch and try to put any difficult incident behind you.
- Giving her refuge does not mean you have to ignore difficult behavior forever.
- Take the waiting out of wanting—anticipate her feelings and volunteer the comfort that you can see she needs.
- Take the opportunity, at a neutral, stress-free time, to tell her openly that your home will always be her refuge if she needs it.

Teachers

- Some girls find it hard to admit errors and may get themselves into increasing trouble by offering multiple and increasingly thin excuses. Try to intervene and forgive before a student digs herself in too deep.
- If a pupil relies on school for her refuge, make sure it's available.
- Help everyone, through class discussion, to be aware of everyone's need for refuge from time to time. Discuss whom they may go to, when and where, and why it can be important to seek refuge.
- Although girls are often open with friends, some may be friendless. Peer counseling can make girls more willing to seek refuge within school.

10 Make her feel she belongs

Human beings have a profound need to feel they belong somewhere and to someone. Your daughter's first need will be to feel loved by the two people who made her or who are responsible for her. As she grows, the more friends, groups, and institutions she feels a bond with and can identify with, the deeper her sense of self will be. When she fits in somewhere, it tells her something about who she is, that she's not alone and not a freak. Belonging to a family, a social or ethnic group, a club, a school or place of worship also signifies she is wanted, accepted and acceptable. It provides her with some guidelines for who she is and how she should behave.

If a girl grows up without any sense of belonging—to a family, school and so on—if she feels rejected through, for example, heavy criticism, she is likely to seek acceptance and a sense of membership elsewhere. She may seek others who have opted out of trying to please and instead gain pleasure and status in dangerous ways.

Parents

• Tell your daughter family stories, so that she knows her own and your roots.

• Include her in as many family activities as possible.

• Understand how fashion and uniforms can be symbols of belonging, especially for younger girls, and help her to "fit in"—provided she does not become dependent and that her needs can be accommodated by your family budget.

• Be on the look-out for signs of "aloneness." Suggest that your daughter join a sports or social club or youth group if she spends too much time on her own.

Teachers

• Circle discussions and similar arrangements can reinforce group identity and make each child feel she's an equal member of the class.

• Stable groups allow a clear identity to form. Staff and student changes and re-groupings can be minimized for girls who may be especially vulnerable.

• A class with high student turnover throughout the year will need constant efforts to re-establish the group's coherence.

• Girls who have attended several schools will be especially needy.

11 Allow her some privacy

My mother wanted to know everything about me, especially how I thought about things. It drove me nuts and I felt kind of invaded. One day I screamed, "Stop trying to get inside my head!"

As girls grow up, they like to mark their growing sense of independence and separateness by acquiring space and time to keep to and for themselves. Parents should not get unduly upset when their daughter tries to mark out territory that belongs exclusively to her, from which they seem excluded. This territory might be her bedroom, it might be a "secret society" with friends or it might be a diary. Later, it might be her social or sexual life. The more appropriate personal and private territory she is gradually allowed as she grows up, the less likely she is to take over and lock you out of areas to which you need to maintain access.

If a girl's need for privacy and autonomy is not met, and it becomes a craving, she may be drawn into the manipulative, secret and life-threatening process of controlling what she eats.

Parents

• Respect your daughter's need for some aspects of her life to belong to her alone. When she's very young, you can give her a drawer, shelf or part of the yard for her sole use.

• Some children who feel invaded or controlled by their parents will create a private world that involves a lot of fantasy or secrecy, to the point of habitually stealing or lying.

• Never read her personal diary. If you suspect behavior that may require your intervention, ask her directly.

• If snacking or school become her only private space, try to give her more privacy elsewhere—in her head, in her room or private time after school.

Teachers

• School is a crowded and public place in which both action and participation are valued highly. Girls whose home space is confined and similarly crowded may need to seek their privacy within school.

• To respect and meet this need, offer quiet rooms or, for younger children, a quiet corner in the classroom.

• Girls who don't participate in certain lessons may be taking private time.

• Be careful that girls who genuinely need quiet time do not become progressively withdrawn.

12 Encourage a self-regarding femininity

Despite the fact that girls today have opportunities previous generations only dreamed of, a heritage and history of suppression, denigration and self-denigration remain and do not easily disappear. Men and women, and boys and girls, may indeed be different—physiologically, psychologically, and hormonally—but these differences do not, and should not, translate into rigid roles or fixed assumptions about status and worth.

Girls are entitled to grow up feeling proud, not ashamed, of who they are. They should be able to look at themselves in the mirror and not only like who they see, because they know they count for something to somebody, but also feel excited at the prospect of exploring whatever talents they possess. Femininity is a given laid down by genes; it is not qualified by either looks or body shape.

Every girl must be encouraged to have a regard for herself that encompasses her gender but also respects her autonomy and the potential this gives her to influence her world.

Parents

- Bolster your daughter's integrity: Help her to be honest with herself and you, to trust her own judgment and to have ideals and live by them.
- Reinforce her individuality, not her inclination to follow the herd.
- Encourage her to care for others, but not to deny her own needs in the process or to define herself solely as a "giver."
- Try not to belittle womanhood or any mother who chooses to either stay at home or work full time. Allow your daughter to choose for herself.
- Don't tolerate hurtful talk or cliquey behavior simply because you think "girls will be girls."

Teachers

- Encourage a school-wide policy of zero tolerance of hostile or abusive talk, whether it be sarcasm and ridicule or violent and aggressive language.
- Avoid scheduling community service or environmental activities as an alternative to sports. No girl or boy should have to choose between being athletic and contributing to the community.
- Ensure plenty of class discussion to raise awareness of and encourage caring about gender issues.

13 Support her when she's under stress

Contrary to popular belief, stress is not something only adults suffer. In fact, children get a double dose, from events in their own lives, such as bullying, academic pressure or friendship problems, and the added effect of adult stress when parents become preoccupied and less tolerant. Given that children have less experience of life and of themselves to trust that "normality" will resume, they are likely to be more confused and disoriented by stress than an adult—not less.

Events that may destabilize a child include separations from those close to her, including friends and pets; anything that will change the way she sees herself or how she imagines other people see her; and changes to either routines or relationships that upset familiar patterns.

If your daughter is unhappy for longer than you would expect; becomes aggressive, withdrawn or socially isolated; sleeps badly; develops stomach and other pains or a strong thirst; loses weight or concentration; or becomes more dependent, she may be distressed and you should take action.

Parents

- If your daughter seems upset, spend more time with her and make sure she gets plenty of sleep.
- Take her worries seriously, even if they seem insignificant to you.
- Keep her informed about changes and decisions, so that she feels less out of control. Keep regular routines going to reinforce her sense of security.
- Giving emotional support is tiring. Get more rest and take some breaks so that you can continue to give what it takes.
- Remember, stress undermines self-esteem.

Teachers

- Look out for signs of stress, such as deteriorating work; changes in behavior; frequent visits to the nurse; becoming more isolated, tearful and sensitive to criticism; leaving class to get books or visit the bathroom; destroying their own work.
- Find the time to talk to a student if you are concerned about her.
- Share your worries with relevant colleagues and contact the girl's home if your concerns continue.
- Be aware that your own stress may make you more vulnerable to and less tolerant of challenges from students or colleagues.

CHAPTER 3

Deepening Her Self-Knowledge and Self-Awareness

For your daughter to be able to stand up for herself, she has to have a clear concept of her "self"—that is, who she is and how she feels. For too long, and in too many cultures, the ideal woman has been somebody who practices self-denial, in one or both senses: 1) She denies herself things occasionally, in terms of consumption or fulfillment, in order to meet the needs of other people, or 2) in a more extreme form, she is denied any self-expression or identity, in which case her idea of who she is is unclear. If she spends her life deferring first to her parents and brothers, then to her husband, a girl will have merely a reflected sense of self that is as intangible as a mirage. To grow up with reliable self-confidence—with a self-generated, concrete, reliable and resilient sense of self-worth—your daughter will need not only to have plenty of opportunities to define herself and discover her potential, but also to be acknowledged and treated as an individual worthy of respect.

Before babies learn to talk and think, they know themselves only through their feelings. Throughout life, our perceptions and passions continue to be important to self-understanding. The fact that certain things frustrate us, make us happy, interest us, excite us, upset or hurt us defines our personality. Many parents find it easy to let their daughters continue to express their feelings freely, but not all. Any child who is forced to cut herself off from her instincts and intuition must discard a part of her inner self, which can create a void. If her feelings are constantly denied and distorted, she may find it easier to ignore her own feelings and passions as a child, and harder to empathize with others as an adult.

Self-awareness and self-knowledge are also practical attributes that contribute to motivation and learning. To progress, a girl has to know what she is capable of and what she still needs to know in order to master a skill or reach an objective. Self-knowledge and reflection are key prerequisites for self-direction. On an inspirational and intuitive level, it is the ability to look inside and know herself that will give your daughter a sense of awe and wonder, an appreciation of beauty and an understanding of the inner world of other people, on which lasting and intimate relationships depend.

The play therapist Virginia Axline has written, "The child must first learn self-respect and a sense of dignity that grows out of his increasing self-understanding before he can learn to respect the personalities and rights and differences of others." In order to be sensitive to other people's sensitivities, we first must understand ourselves. Those who live and work with girls have a duty, then, to develop the girls' sense of self by heightening their self-awareness and self-knowledge.

14 Offer choices

As adults, we are fortunate to have a lot of choice. It gives us more control over our lives. Common sense tells us that children should also have choices, but how much, when and, just as important, why?

In a world of multiple and unfamiliar choices, girls need to be able to make informed and responsible decisions. Your daughter will do this better if she understands her own preferences, is sure enough about them to resist outside pressure and can think through the consequences of her choices on herself and others. Any adult who lives and works with girls should help develop these thinking and reflective skills whenever possible.

Choice is important because it gives children some scope to influence what happens to them and keeps them from feeling used and powerless. By helping them define what they like and want, choice also helps sharpen their sense of self.

Parents

• Younger children can be given appropriate choices about what they wear, what they play, whom they play with and what story they hear or read at bedtime.

• Encourage choice with open-ended questions: "How about playing with . . . ?" —avoid answering the question before they do.

• Older girls can have some choice about when and where they do their homework, what (though not how much) TV they watch, what they spend their allowance on and so on.

Teachers

• Respect a student's decisions: Don't ask her what she wants, then ignore her reply.

• Choices help to manage behavior in the classroom. For example: "You can stop talking and fooling around, or you can have detention; it's your choice."

15 Manage choices

In larger families, meeting everyone's whims and wishes can be impossible. It's not good for them, or you. Too much choice can undermine a girl's sense of self: Never having to make true choices, she won't discover what she really likes best. She can become confused and unhappy with too many choices about too many things and she won't feel her parent is taking overall responsibility.

Too much choice has other down sides: It may encourage your daughter to control and manipulate situations. It won't help her to live with the reality of disappointment and may encourage her to become selfish and insensitive to other people's needs. It can take responsibility from her because she can always say, "Sorry, wrong choice—I'll take this one instead," if she doesn't like the consequences of her decision. Endless choice can also lead to arguments: If all her wants are satisfied quickly, she may push and push to the point where you explode.

To help a girl strengthen and deepen her self-knowledge and self-esteem, limit and manage her choices.

Parents

- Managed choice means either/or decisions. You put limits on the choices by giving her options to choose from that you can support.
- Limited choice means giving her choices no more than a few times a day.
- Avoid open-ended choices; on a cold day, it's better to say to a young child, "Would you like to wear your jacket or sweater?" than to leave her dress choice wide open. Another example is to have only two or three items to choose from for breakfast.
- Make sure the choices you offer are ones you can make happen.
- Girls should not normally be in charge of how the whole family spends its time.

Teachers

- Choice is motivating. Students who are given some choice about what they do and how they do it are usually more committed to their work.
- Include aspects of choice within project work—not so much that it becomes hard to start, but enough to let a student make it her own.
- Where there is little scope for choice in classwork, try additional activities that focus on choice, such as "If I could be a food/tree/color/musical instrument/car/country/piece of furniture/an animal, I'd be a . . . , because . . ."

16 Don't impose your views

My father was autocratic. He couldn't discuss anything. He just stated his view and declared all others to be uninformed and stupid. He tried to tell me what to think and how to do everything. I ended up not paying attention to anything he said.

It is easy to become so convinced by your own status and wisdom as a parent that you dish out declarations, decisions and assertions without realizing it, squashing your daughter's growing need to explore her own views on any matter. Too much criticism or praise, or excessive use of rewards, can do the same—you are asking and encouraging her to live by your views and values.

Preteen girls are considered to be suggestible: They like to please and conform. Do not take advantage of this; make a special effort to foster your daughter's individuality and self-awareness. Later, when girls define what they're not before they explore who they are, it is very common for them to reject their parents' values. They should be free to cross that road without being run over.

Parents

• Invite your daughter's views: Say, for example, "I like it, but it's what you think that's important," not "That's great, don't you think?"; and "What did you think of that TV show?" not "That show was garbage."

• Think carefully about the things you care about, and be aware that your daughter is likely to target these as she asserts her independence. If she does, don't take it personally.

• Even with a younger child, the more you push your views and values and assume she should share them, the more likely she is to reject them.

Teachers

• Encourage students to think ahead about what might happen next—for example, in a science experiment, ask instead of tell them what they are about to see.

• Resist the temptation to save time by delivering the standard arguments for and against something in classwork. Always seek students' views, to develop their confidence and thinking skills.

• If you get involved in working out a conflict between two girls, don't impose solutions on them but encourage them to devise their own.

• In general debates, keep your views to yourself to allow students to explore theirs. (This does not mean you cannot question and challenge gently.)

17 Give her feelings space in your world

As a girl, I was forced to live on an emotional plateau, never allowed to express boundless joy or the depths of sadness. Being constrained by moderation in all things suffocated me and I almost lost myself. My own daughter skips around the house when she's happy, and I love to see it.

If someone said to you, "You have no right to feel that!" you would probably become angry. Children also get upset when their feelings are denied. We now understand that feelings are as important as thoughts in the development of our children as unique and giving human beings. If we reject our daughter's feelings, we reject her as she experiences herself.

Feelings used to be viewed as somehow inferior to thoughts, more closely associated with instinct and animals, something that governed us when we were primitive, not civilized and sophisticated. We now know that they play an important role in conjunction with conscious thought, partly to assist survival when life is threatened and partly as a way to understand the situations in which we find ourselves.

Parents

- If you can accept your daughter's feelings, she can learn to live with, manage, enjoy or work through them herself.
- Help her ask for what she needs: "I think you're feeling upset. Would a hug help?" can free her to say, "I'm feeling down, and I'd like some comfort."
- You accept her feelings when you accept her apologies. You could model this behavior along these lines: "I was sharp with you because I had an awful day today. I'm sorry."
- Feelings of jealousy, anger, frustration and resentment should be accepted, not punished or denied; however, while it's fine to feel, it's not fine to hurt someone because of the way you feel.

Teachers

- Give girls sentences to complete, such as, "I'm happiest when . . ."; "When I get angry, I . . ."; " I feel most important when . . ."; "I feel frustrated when . . ."; "I tend to give up when . . . ."
- Brainstorm emotions: Invite the class to discuss how they feel about or see something. Explore words that express emotions: for example, frustration, powerlessness, anger, rage. Students can discuss events that trigger certain emotions and decide whether the feeling anyone describes fits the one under discussion.
- Give younger children a feelings log book, in which they write, at set (and free) times, their reactions to work assignments, school, events or people.

18 Tell her her story

Once when you were little, you got so angry that you hid behind the couch with some scissors and cut a hole in it! Then it was my turn to be angry!

Young children love to be told stories about themselves—when they were babies, how older brothers and sisters reacted when they were born and so on. These anecdotes give your daughter a history. They are the puzzle pieces of her life that she can't reach but that she needs for a complete picture of herself.

Older children like to hear different stories—about their parents' childhood and school days, or the antics of aunts and uncles. Such tales deepen a girl's sense of belonging because she will understand better what it is she belongs to. Each story will act as a thread that creates continuity. Like a spider's web, the more threads she has, the stronger she will feel.

You need to talk about difficult times, too. There will be gaps in her history if particular incidents are left out.

Parents

• Get out your family photos occasionally and talk about the people and events they show. This activity fills gaps in her understanding of family history and can generate laughter, lead to other linked issues, reinforce your daughter's identity and increase her confidence in the future.

• Regularly recall past holidays, birthday parties, special treats or vacations that were fun and brought the family together.

• Keep mementos such as your daughter's first shoes and her favorite toys, books and clothes so that you can revisit the past and show her it's important to you.

• Discuss problems, don't bury them. She has a right to information about herself so that she can make sense of her world.

Teachers

• Personal life-lines: In a group, discuss the many different experiences that are important in each student's life, what made these events significant and how the child felt at the time. Ask each child to draw a vertical line on a large sheet of paper. The line represents their life from birth (bottom) to the present (top). They then write in their own personal events, positive and negative, on either side of the line.

• Not everyone has a happy family story to tell. Focus on both good and bad, happy and sad experiences to ensure a full and realistic picture that leaves no one out.

• Make sure you include all types of family and caring arrangements when you discuss family matters with your class.

19 Encourage the practice of reflection

Reflection means standing outside oneself, looking in at what has happened, and asking questions like "Why?", "How?" and "What if?" *To reflect* means "to consult with oneself, go back in thought." Reflection entails reliving your experiences and having a silent conversation with yourself to identify connections and understand them. It increases self-awareness and helps you to make sense of your life, take control and introduce changes.

Reflection is beneficial because thinking backward is the first step to thinking forward, which is important for learning, sustaining relationships, managing conflict without violence and planning one's life. If a girl cannot reflect on what she has said and done, assess the good and the bad, and realize what she might need to change, she cannot develop and make progress in anything. Becoming aware of how she feels and behaves helps her to understand other people's feelings and actions, and therefore to anticipate possible problems in relationships. Understanding her past will help her face the future.

Parents

• Recap and reflect on the day's events with your daughter as part of the evening routine. Invite her to think aloud about both its good and bad aspects.

• Show her how to reflect by reflecting on your own day: "I wonder if I could have done that another way?" or "I really felt excited/angry when it happened."

• Ensure that your daughter reads fiction; when possible, discuss the story's events and characters.

• Encourage drama, imaginative play and dressing up, depending on her age.

Teachers

• Ensure that girls read fiction regularly as well as nonfiction. Discuss the story line and characters.

• Introduce role reversal in drama to explore alternative experiences.

• Ask each child to write down two negative descriptions of herself on one piece of paper and two positive descriptions of herself on another. Transfer them to a large board and discuss them. Ask, for example, "Are you always irritating? If not, when are you, and why?" to help girls reflect upon and reject negative labels that they may assume without question.

20 Arrange relaxation and quiet time

Most girls have times when they like to be on the go and let off steam, but every girl also needs to be able to slow down when the situation or person requires it and to feel comfortable within herself when she does stop. It's good to be active, but being bored isn't a crime. Children are more likely to explore and develop their inner selves when they are quiet and they should not panic at the prospect.

Quiet time means the chance to be calm, to wind down, to relax or even escape. Quiet time also means being peaceful, at rest and happy to be alone. Each girl has her own way to unwind. One will prefer to flop in front of the television. Another will choose to play with a pet. Some like to relax while listening to music. Others will be happy to reflect as they draw or doodle.

Being quiet at these times gives a girl the chance to let her thoughts roam, to find out what is inside her and learn to be content with and within herself.

Parents

- Discover your daughter's mechanisms for winding down and encourage her to use them, especially after school or when she's been very active—times when she may find it hard to "come down."
- Respect the older girls' need for their own quiet space, which may not be within your home if it is a busy place.
- Encourage quiet togetherness: Watch TV or a video with your daughter, make time for morning snuggling in bed if she is still young enough to enjoy it, or sometimes drive her to her friends' homes.

Teachers

- Simple breathing and relaxation exercises can work well with grade school children. Older girls may need more encouragement and may find yoga or another relaxation technique more acceptable.
- Have a clear ending planned for each class, especially those in which there has been a lot of activity. Use this time to recap and encourage pupils to reflect on what they have learned.

21 Explain your thoughts and feelings

"Children need models more than they need critics." So said the French philosopher Joubert. Your daughter will learn to identify and express her thoughts and feelings safely and comfortably if she sees you doing so.

One mistaken but common view of assertiveness is that thoughts and views should be presented in a commanding and dictatorial fashion as "the truth." This denies the possibility that others, including children, may see things differently, which may lead to conflict.

You should explain, not assert, thoughts and arguments, with the possible exception of key matters of discipline. A useful principle is to assert your right to be heard, not your view of the world. Inner strength is based on tolerance and respect, not domination. Taking this stance is also immensely liberating: If you don't need to dominate, you don't need to be right each and every time.

Parents

• If you are angry, upset, or frustrated, say so and explain why. Don't just shout.

• When you explain your reactions to your daughter's actions, it helps her learn to anticipate, predict and become more thoughtful and sensitive. And she learns to be responsible for her behavior.

• Tell her how you arrived at a particular decision: for example, "I first thought this, then I realized that, so I decided . . ."

• You alone are responsible for your feelings. Say, "I felt angry when . . .", not "You made me angry."

• If your daughter swears, ask her to find an alternative word to express what she is trying to say, and do the same yourself.

Teachers

• Help your students find the best language with which to express their thoughts and feelings.

• Be a model for this: Try to express your own thoughts appropriately.

• Use phrases that start with "I" to avoid appearing to blame anyone.

• Emotional literacy requires a particular vocabulary. Girls need to discover which words they can use to express their feelings. They will enjoy widening their vocabularies to replace expletives, if the opportunity is presented well.

22 Maintain communication

I thought my daughter was fine. She seemed to deal with her life, though she was alone a lot, and I dealt with mine. We didn't talk much. Then, in the middle of her final exams, she withdrew from everything. Now she won't work, go out or talk. We're in a real mess.

If children and adults don't communicate, the price to pay can be very high indeed. Communication skills lie at the heart of social and emotional health and success, and a girl will not be as comfortable about talking if adults, especially parents, don't talk to her. No conversation implies no interest, which she may interpret as neglect, so family silence can have a devastating impact on her self-esteem, her sense of self-worth and her trust in future relationships.

Family conversations will also help your daughter be comfortable with expressing her views in front of other adults in positions of authority as well as her peers. It will increase her confidence and help her to stand her ground with professionals and authorities in the future.

Parents

- Keep talking, even if it feels uncomfortable—the more you do it, the easier it will become.
- Try to eat with your daughter as often as possible. If this happens only occasionally, forget table manners and other controversial subjects. Swallow hard if she challenges you, and don't rise to the bait.
- If you want to take issue with something, start with the word "I": for example, "I'm not happy about doing all the housework and I'd like some help."
- Always stop and listen.
- If you have to be away, for work or for pleasure, give her your undivided time when you return to touch base with her again.

Teachers

- Withdrawn or silent students reduce demands on teachers, but never assume that they are doing just fine.
- Although quiet students may simply be taking time out, be vigilant: Identify any long-term patterns; consult your colleagues; talk informally and socially to such students; and step in sooner rather than later if you are still concerned.
- Ensure that lesson plans entail a variety of exercises that encourage involvement and include work in small groups.
- In all lessons, nurture the essential skills of communication: reflection, listening and tolerance for others.

23 Encourage self-assessment

Although our children like to know they have pleased us, what we should try to encourage in them from the start is the confidence to evaluate and praise themselves.

Girls are inclined to undervalue their work and worth and are typically self-effacing. For some, this may help them put in the extra effort they believe is required to improve their results, but this can reinforce the view that "I only did well because I worked—I'm not really that good." However, with support and guidance, they can learn to assess themselves and their skills realistically and do themselves justice. The particular danger time is the early teens. Girls' self-confidence dips noticeably around the age of fourteen.

The sting of criticism and skepticism about praise are removed when the evaluation comes from themselves. Self-assessment is important because it is central to independent learning.

Parents

• Avoid being generally critical and judgmental so that your daughter does not learn to depend on your opinion and lose faith in her own.

• When your daughter asks what you think of something she has done—a painting, an essay, an achievement, a music piece—turn the question back to her. What matters, ultimately, is what she thinks of her effort. Encouraging her to trust herself is crucial.

• Minimize criticism, especially in relation to a girl's looks and abilities, because it will force her increasingly to seek approval from you.

Teachers

• Girls can be encouraged to assess each other's work, in pairs, as a first step to learning how to be honest about their own work.

• If preschool children can work well with a "plan, do, then review" approach, older girls can certainly handle this, too.

• Full and accurate feedback is vital: At the end of any work, a student can assess its merit, then you can detail why and how it did, or did not, meet the standards for that assessment.

• Once self-assessment becomes frequent and normal, there will be no excuse for a girl to underestimate her abilities.

24 Hear the sound of silence

Between fourteen and sixteen, our daughter hardly spoke to us, except for yelling! She spent hours in her room and became almost a recluse. I was really worried. Then her skin started to clear and, like a butterfly, she emerged more confident and began to socialize again.

In the end, this parent trusted her instinct and everything turned out okay, but take care. If your daughter withdraws and stops talking, it doesn't necessarily mean you can assume she's all right, because she might not be. It could be a sign of unhappiness and depression.

However, your daughter does not have to talk all the time. Silence can mean she feels comfortable and does not need to fill every moment with words. It can be understood as quiet togetherness. The important thing is not to ignore it if a girl becomes quiet. Hear the silence, reflect on it, accept it for a time, see if you can find out what she is doing when she is on her own. And step in if you believe she is withdrawn from others as well as you, and if there are other signs of problems.

Parents

- Keep talking—about things that won't start an argument—but don't force your daughter to respond.
- Suggest you do something together that doesn't rely on talking, such as swimming, bowling or going to the movies.
- Be aware of danger signs, such as leaving late for or missing school frequently, changes in her eating patterns, unusual smells that could indicate solitary drug or alcohol use, or any drop in the standard of her personal care.

Teachers

- Small-group activities encourage participation and offer less chance to hide behind silence.
- A girl who clams up in the classroom may be afraid of making mistakes or she may be distracted by problems—it's important to find out why she isn't talking.
- Try to include activities that require everyone to participate.

CHAPTER 4

Giving Her a Positive View of Herself

The twenty-first century is likely to be characterized by considerable change and uncertainty. To manage this successfully, a girl must see herself and her capabilities in a positive light. This does not mean she must see herself as perfect—indeed, it is better if she does not.

If your daughter feels sure of herself, she will find it much easier to resist, or at least handle responsibly, undue academic pressure, peer coercion and the temptation to use alcohol, drugs and sex inappropriately. As an adult, her "can do" attitude will help her to stand up for herself, and she will be better able to manage her finances, relationships, children and career. However, if she sees herself as a source of problems, mistakes, disappointment, pain and distress, she will lack the confidence to take on challenges or commitments.

So how can adults help to create "can do" girls who are motivated, enthusiastic, and full of optimism? It is vital to demonstrate that your daughter is important to you and to remain supportive, give plenty of positive feedback, extend her horizons and do all the things that will make her feel loved and wanted. But it is also crucial that you minimize the blame, nagging and fault-finding that convey disappointment.

Without intending to, you can send harmful messages about how likeable and competent she is, with damaging consequences for her mental health, stability, self-esteem and motivation.

Constant criticism will make her feel she can never please, that something is fundamentally wrong with her. She will always be looking over her shoulder, wondering which of her actions will be disapproved of next. This undermines confidence, initiative and morale; so do shouting, unwarranted blame and routine harsh, erratic punishment.

We find many excuses for our damaging words and may say that she deserved it. We may see any challenging reactions from her as a sign that the words did not hurt—not realizing that the shield she raises is a protective fiction. If she reacts with hostility, we often see it as rejection and think why should we bother to be pleasant to her anyway? If we sense any hurt, we may tell ourselves it's time she grew up. But a girl who "cannot take" constructive criticism has often taken a bucketful of it and should be given no more if she is to have any energy left to protect her self-respect.

Neglect hurts, too. When parents lead lives in which their daughter hardly features, or give her more freedom than is right for her age, she may interpret this as indifference. What a girl needs is not her parent's declaration that she is loved, but the demonstration of this love, through actions and words, in a way that she can appreciate.

25 Understand her differences

Every girl is different. She will feel things differently, play differently, think differently, learn differently and enjoy different things. These unique characteristics define who she is as a human being, regardless of her gender. A girl will have a clearer appreciation of the different elements within herself if the adults who know her well put what they see into words and encourage her to do the same.

To take the analogy of an artist's palette, the more "colors," or traits and talents, that are utilized, the more interesting and colorful the painting. Too often, parents see their daughters in black and white, not in color. They are either "good" and "successful" or "difficult" and "hopeless." To remain proud, happy and confident, girls need to view themselves as multidimensional and multicolored, having a variety of positive personality traits and abilities.

Parents

• Fill in your daughter's "personality palette." Write down her likes and dislikes: what she likes to eat or won't eat; her favorite games, sports, and activities; the clothes she likes; what she's good at; the places she likes to go; how she works best.

• Be positive: Traits you view as negative are probably the reverse side of positive ones. For example, she may stand up for herself with friends but be "too assertive" with you.

• Tell her what you see. For example: "I really like the way you . . ." or "You're very caring/sensitive/good with your hands, aren't you?"

Teachers

• Consult with other staff members to determine specific strengths and weaknesses of any student you find "difficult."

• Be aware of different learning styles and vary lessons appropriately.

• Ask your students what learning styles they prefer.

• Ask students to get into small groups. Select one student in turn, then have the rest of the group tell her all the strengths and unique features they see in her (no put-downs are allowed). One person should record the contributions, listing ten to fifteen strengths for each person.

26 Don't compare her to others

For some girls, living in the shadow of a brother or sister is a nightmare that persists for the rest of their lives. A girl may never quite shake off the humiliation and feeling of inferiority. Comments such as "Your brother would not have produced work like that" or "You're not as talented as your sister" can ruin pride and kill ambition. Friends, too, can be used (or rather abused) as a model for her to measure up to: "Why can't you dress nicely, like Tammy?" These taunts, far from acting as spurs, tend to taint the childhood of those who suffer them. Comparisons undermine confidence and fuel conflict.

Even handing out equal praise can be limiting. Saying, "She's the brainy one in the family and he's the athlete" may give each child something to be proud of, but will also make it less likely that either will explore their potential in the other's field of interest. Although brothers and sisters may be genuinely different, they also make themselves different to create their own territory. When skills become territories, children can become tribal. And don't forget that comparisons with any other girl's body shape or weight should never leave your lips.

Parents

- Celebrate difference. Every child is entitled to be different, look different and respond differently, because each one is unique.
- Make it clear that there is room for more than one artist, pianist or athlete in the family.
- Discourage any family focus on body image or shape, and don't compare your daughter's body with anyone else's, favorably or unfavorably.
- Don't compare your daughter with how you were or what you did at her age. She is herself, not you.

Teachers

- Positively value each child as an individual. Never use references to siblings to disparage or coerce work.
- Be especially supportive of originality and creativity, because these are the manifestations of a girl's unique self.
- Competition promotes anxiety. The only constructive comparison is with an individual's last performance or piece of work.

27 Respect her feelings

Feelings are fundamental. They make us who we are. Although in general, parents will find feelings such as fear and anxiety easier to accept in girls than in boys, there is a danger that the pursuit of equality and success will tempt parents to restrain such feelings in their daughters as well as their sons. There is another reason many adults want girls to stop being "emotional": The sooner children can control their fears and feelings, the sooner parents can stop having to "waste" their time responding to them. Fear of the dark, of water, of spiders, fear of losing friendships, of failure, of nightmares and bogeymen test parents' patience. They try to respond with rational arguments to a fear that is actually irrational. For your daughter, the fear may not be on the rational spectrum—it may instead be purely emotional, and the two don't mix.

Whether they feel delight or disappointment, fear or fury, joy or jealousy, girls are entitled to have their emotions acknowledged and respected by their parents and caregivers, because this is the route through which they experience the essence of what is themselves.

Parents

• Respect your daughter's fears and anxieties, hopes and dreams, even (and especially) when they seem silly or irrational to you.

• Share her delights and disappointments.

• Acknowledge and describe how she might be feeling, so that she develops a language that will help her to understand her emotions.

Teachers

• Fear of failure explains a wide spectrum of behavior that obstructs learning. Encourage students to be open about their fears.

• At all ages, drama and role-playing can allow both girls and boys to explore emotions safely.

• Some girls are naturally intuitive and aware. Group debate and discussion will help those with less insight to learn from those with more.

• Reading fiction is an effective way to explore experiences and consider their impact.

28 Listen with both eyes

My dad doesn't really listen to me. I'd love him, one day, to put his newspaper down or turn off the TV when I'm talking to him. I feel like a nobody.

Listening involves looking just as much as hearing. When you listen with half an ear, it usually means you are concentrating on something else you are doing, not looking at your daughter. When you look at her, three things happen: First, you have to stop what you are doing, so that your full attention is directed at her; second, eye contact with her helps you to fix your thoughts on her and what she has to tell you; third, you are able to read her body language and facial expressions, which will help you to understand anything that lies behind the words.

When parents and teachers don't listen properly, or at all, they are saying, in effect, that they and their business are more important. If a girl is ignored, she will feel insignificant and undermined. She will not feel comfortable with herself and her self-esteem cannot possibly flourish.

Parents

- When your daughter wants to tell you something, use your eyes first, not your ears. Stop what you are doing and focus on her.
- Look at her facial expression and watch for any hidden meaning in her body language. Notice how she is standing or sitting and her tone of voice.
- Let her know you are taking her seriously: "This sounds important. I think I'd better sit down and really listen to you."

Teachers

- Show awareness: "My antennae tell me there is more to this story than you are telling me."
- Teach students about body language and be vigilant about its application in all oral activities in the classroom.
- Provide plenty of opportunity for girls in discussions, debates and presentations to listen to and respect each other's contributions.

29 See with both ears

Like listening with both eyes, seeing with both ears is about helping adults to be more sensitive to a girl's inner world, which is as important to her as the outer, more visible one. Both influence the quality of her self-confidence, listening being more important.

You get a glimpse of what might be happening inside your daughter by listening to her "self-talk"—what she expresses about herself. Adolescent girls are particularly prone to run themselves down. For example, a girl may seem to be doing well at school, and to have aced a particular test. However, she may respond to the result by saying, "That was a fluke. I didn't deserve it," or "I'll probably fail next time." Her words show that, inside, she doubts herself. Similarly, she may have plenty of friends, but if one backs out on doing something with her and she retorts, "She's probably had a better invitation," it indicates a tendency to belittle herself with negative self-talk.

Parents

- Listen for times when she talks badly about herself and rephrase her comments to make them accurate and positive.
- Try to keep a record of what your daughter says and how often she makes self-deprecating comments, even if she's joking, to help you recognize any pattern or the scale of the problem.
- Simply denying a child's self-criticism won't have much impact. Turn a generalization into a specific, so that "I'm never any good!" becomes "You did not do as well as you wanted this time." Or repeat several times that what you see is different: "I think you're quick to see the point/amusing and fun to be with" or "I see you as someone who . . ."

Teachers

- Be positive. Discourage negativity and challenge "I can't do this" assertions.
- Encourage self-evaluation tasks in which students write about their performance and highlight areas where they believe they performed best.
- If a girl says she's no good and knows nothing, draw a horizontal line with "knowing nothing" at one end and "knowing everything" at the other. Invite her to mark the appropriate place that represents how much she really knows. She'll realize that she certainly knows something.

30 Respect her play

As a child, I had a wonderful time, making up stories, getting into minor trouble, spending hours outside with my friends.

Fortunately, girls love to play: Play is essential to the development of self-esteem and confidence. They are particularly good at developing story lines as they make believe and play act with their friends. Through play, girls find out who they are. Through the choices they make about what to play or do, whom to play with and so on, they gradually flesh out their idea of who they are and gain an identity—two essential steps in building self-esteem. Through play, girls also discover what they can do, because play develops verbal, social, manual, planning, problem-solving, negotiation and physical skills, which enhance their self-confidence and their ability to socialize and make friends.

Finally, through safely managed independent play, girls gradually realize that they can handle life on their own.

Parents

• Encourage your daughter to play: with you, with her friends, on her own, indoors and outdoors.

• Let her choose what to play most of the time.

• Respect her play by giving her notice of when she must stop, instead of expecting her to stop the moment you say so. And don't spoil her fantasies by teasing or ridiculing her.

• Pretending, dressing up, drawing and creative games are all important because they help girls to become spontaneous, imaginative and creative, which helps them to do well at school.

• Help your daughter to become familiar with computers, for they are the way of the present and future.

Teachers

• Show respect for students' hobbies and interests, and utilize these for individual presentations and projects.

• Role-play and improvisation can be fun and can provide a valuable release for girls.

• Though play is important, there are places and times when it is appropriate and places and times when the fun must stop. Build in winding-down time after intense activity to help mark the boundary between the two.

• Encourage girls to extend their play repertoire to include action games as well as quiet activities.

31 Let her impress you

All children get a boost when someone they admire is clearly impressed by something they have done. They puff up with extra confidence and pleasure. It does their self-confidence a lot of good. Showing that you are impressed is, of course, a form of praise, and a very effective one, which avoids some of the pitfalls associated with praise.

Being impressed is straightforward, open and takes away some of the judgment implicit in other forms of praise. Most important, it is unconditional. "I am really impressed!" or "That was impressive!" says it all—no "ifs" or "buts" to qualify it or detract from the core message. There is nothing grudging about being impressed!

To say you are impressed also clears the air of competition. Some parents feel they should be stronger, better and more successful than their offspring and need to prove it. But being impressed by your daughter doesn't mean that she has got the better of you, and it won't stop her from trying; it simply shows admiration, which is what girls thirst to receive.

Parents

• Involve your daughter in real tasks, working alongside you: Ask her to help you fix things, sort things, decide things, clean things, then say, "Wow, you were good. I'm impressed!"

• Show that you respect her skills and her views: "You're good at fixing things. Can you help me with this?"

• Give her appropriate responsibilities, so that she can test herself, develop her skills and feel trustworthy—then let her know she has achieved this.

• When she's little, let her win in little ways, and show how impressed you are.

• You can genuinely admire her computer skills, which probably will be far superior to yours.

Teachers

• Allocate responsibilities, such as reporting back from group discussions, looking up something that will help everyone's classwork, and make it obvious that you are impressed by the outcome.

• Begin questions in the classroom with, for example, "Danielle, you know a lot about this."

• For an impressive piece of work, gauge the appropriate reward, public or private.

32 Fashion her individuality

The media and images affect my life to the point where it gets silly . . . There are always people slimmer and nicer-looking than I am and it knocks my self-esteem. —GIRLPOWER

Very few girls will end up having a model-shaped body or the money to clothe themselves in high fashion every day of the week. The current western cultural focus on body image means that just about every girl will possess some feature that fails to match her expectation or dream, and about which she may become depressed: the shape of her lips, the spread of her buttocks or the size of her eyes. Even grade school-aged girls can become obsessed with their appearance.

But looks are literally superficial—and not even skin-deep when they are cosmetically created. Today, the asset of attractiveness is valued disproportionately highly. If everyone in your family respects social more than physical qualities, accepts difference and shows respect regardless of physique or good looks, your daughter's self-esteem will have a chance to strengthen before it is undermined by her peers.

Parents

• Teach your daughter to honor and care for her body by ensuring that she's clean and healthy and by supporting her when she's sick.

• Don't reinforce fashion-induced stereotypes with sexist remarks.

• Beware of dressing her in fancy clothes, regardless of practicality.

• If it is possible, a regular, limited clothes allowance may help her to avoid being a slave to fashion, because she'll be forced to make practical choices.

• Help her to walk tall, literally and figuratively, because she's proud of who she is inside, regardless of her body shape and wardrobe.

Teachers

• Avoid making comments such as, "You're nice and slim. You can be in the play."

• Avoid team selection systems that leave the larger girls waiting until last.

• Ensure that students are aware of the power of the advertising, fashion and health industries to focus on body image.

• Talk about what is implied by different images of womanhood and manhood, and the role of individual choice and variety.

• Ensure that anyone teaching physical education or nutrition is fully informed of the health needs of growing bodies.

33 Lead her when she's ready

When I got to middle school, I had kind of a crisis. I'd been very active after school, but I realized it had all been organized for me. Suddenly I had to make choices, to become an individual and, because of my parents' involvement, I didn't know who I was or what I really wanted.

Parents can't wait for their children to walk, get out of diapers, read, swim, ride a bike and so on, for many different reasons, some more honorable than others, but this eagerness can undermine a girl's self-esteem.

Girls, like boys, learn best when they are ready. "Ready" means not only being willing—hungry for the knowledge or skill—but also being comfortable and confident about moving forward. They should instinctively know that the necessary prior knowledge is in place to allow them to make sense of what they find. When a girl can influence what she does and when, she begins to know herself intimately and to trust her own judgment, which reinforces her self-esteem.

Parents

• "If it's Wednesday, it must be ballet"—girls are driven, literally and metaphorically, by parents to attend a stream of after-school activities. These keep them busy and give them opportunities to shine, but children get tired. Beware of forcing your daughter into extracurricular pursuits that she doesn't enjoy and at which she's unlikely to succeed.

• Avoid pushing her to progress too soon. If you push too hard, she may actually lose ground.

Teachers

• Encourage "mastery learning": Give students goals and guidance on how to proceed, show assessment criteria, and encourage them to manage themselves within these guidelines. Mastery learning programs are particularly effective with weaker students.

• When a child is motivated, her work improves. Try to enhance each individual's motivation to encourage self-development.

• Girls are often happy to work on their own, but if a student seems to be stuck, a collaborative group-work situation may help her to move on.

34 Accept her friends

Friends boost my confidence because they know me best.

Friendships are extremely important to girls. Friends help her feel she belongs and validate her, because they tell her she is liked and is likeable. They frequently share her interests, help her fill her time, add fun to her life and help her create an identity. She thinks, "I am friends with this type of person, so I am also like this." Real friends offer loyalty and support when things go wrong. In other words, they can play a crucial part in building her identity, confidence and social skills as well as providing safety in numbers, provided it is the "right crowd."

A girl's friends become so close that they are almost an extension of her—if you reject them, you reject her. This makes it extra hard if you want to suggest she's made the wrong choice. If her friends seem to subvert your plans, challenge your values and cause you concern, think very carefully before you try to exclude them. They may simply be normal adolescents needing to break away. Talk to your daughter before you forbid anything or your forbidding may be counterproductive.

Parents

- Invite your daughter's friends to your home or out with your family so that you can get to know them better.
- Find something pleasant to say about them.
- Compliment your daughter on her ability to be a good friend to others.
- If you're worried that her friends are a bad influence, try listing what she's getting from this group. Consider whether these needs can be met in another way. Try also to talk about what she expects from a real friend—respect for her point of view and limits, wanting the best for her and reliability, for example—then let her decide if her current friends have these qualities.

Teachers

- Though you should recognize and respect natural friendships, arrange classroom seating and the composition of groups for project work in ways that encourage mixing and minimize peer pressure, bullying and isolation.
- Explore the issue of friendships and peer pressure through school assemblies and drama. Pose the question, "What makes a good friend?" and invite individuals to write down what qualities they believe they have as a friend to others.
- Work with a group to draw up a "friendship contract": a list of behaviors one would expect from friends.

35 Enter her world, carefully

My mom asked me what my favorite band was at the moment, so I told her and played her a few tracks from a CD. She listened, then wrinkled her nose. She said sorry for not liking them, but I didn't really want her to. It's my music.

It can be hard to judge the amount of involvement any girl wants a parent to have in her life, especially when she is at an age when she needs to become more separate and independent. There are no clear answers—parents must simply remain sensitive to the issue and judge each situation as it arises. But keep in mind two useful principles: Take an interest (without being intrusive) and remember that your prime role is to be your daughter's parent, not her friend. You can be effective and loving without being her best friend, who should be someone from within her peer group.

Parents

- Take an interest in your daughter's hobbies and activities, but don't take them over. They don't have to become your passion, too.
- Give her the space and territory to be separate and different, without cutting yourself off from her.
- Girls frequently use music and dance to explore and establish an individual identity. Ask which band or style is her favorite, but don't make them your favorites, too.
- Sporting events are safe to share and can bring together different generations.

Teachers

- In any class discussions about personal and family matters, acknowledge your students' range of family types and personal experiences, but tread and talk carefully in these areas.
- Think ahead about how you might respond if a student ever becomes upset during discussions of personal issues.

36 Keep criticism to a minimum

When I was a teenager, my mom said that, above the knee, my legs were better than my sister's, but below the knee, my sister's were better than mine. I was furious that she could be that distant, disloyal and judgmental, even though her comments were supposedly even-handed. I never forgot this.

Adults are usually totally unaware of the destructive impact of their careless words, which can do unbelievable damage. Even an occasional clumsy statement made in jest can allow self-doubt to take root, and both girls and boys are more sensitive to criticism than most adults realize. Constant criticism implants not only self-doubt but also guilt and shame about letting parents down. If a girl fails to please, she'll assume she disappoints. Eventually she'll feel useless and rejected, although she will probably hide it well.

In girls, this sense of shame can take dangerous paths, leading them to prove their worth through academic perfectionism or seeking the perfect body—or even to self-harm if they feel totally worthless.

Parents

- Focus on one behavior at a time and ignore the rest. Piling on the criticism will make your daughter resentful and uncooperative.
- Accentuate the positive—focus on what you want done and select one day when you comment on only the good things.
- Try to stop watching and judging, because this implies that you are controlling and mistrustful.
- Banish humiliating phrases (no matter how angry you are), such as, "I can't take you anywhere," "I wish you were never born," and "You make me sick."

Teachers

- Teachers' words can hurt as much as anyone else's.
- Teasing, sarcasm, ridicule, shouting and blame are put-downs that hurt, shame, degrade, damage and humiliate. They sap independence, initiative and morale and are never justified.
- It takes four "praises" to undo the harm of one destructive criticism.
- Turn all of your "don'ts" into "do's".
- Doubts are more cruel than the worst of truths: Keep students' self-doubt at bay, and listen for any tendency to self-criticize.

CHAPTER 5

Demonstrating Care through Love and Rules

We show that we love and care for our girls in different ways. We make sure that our daughter has the right kind of food, so that she grows up strong and healthy. We ensure that she's clean and appropriately clothed, so that she is warm and protected from disease and sickness. We spend time with her, have fun and share our lives with her, which help her to feel loved and wanted. We try to understand and tolerate the mistakes she inevitably makes as she tests herself in the process of gaining skills, confidence and maturity.

However, giving in to your daughter because you can't be bothered to argue won't convince her that you really care—neither will showering her with presents. Having guidelines for behavior in and outside the home that will protect her, you, others and even her physical environment demonstrates your concern for her welfare.

The right kind of discipline will nurture your daughter's self-confidence, because it will make her feel taken care of. It will give her the freedom to explore and take risks within safe boundaries that you carefully define and manage. When she has clear guidelines for behavior and a daily routine, she can relax. She won't have to decide everything for herself, or worry whether she may get into trouble. And when she does behave as expected, life is not only calmer but filled with the warmth of other people's pleasure and approval. Most important, when the adults who take care of her establish appropriate limits for a girl's behavior and are sufficiently involved to notice and watch what she does, she realizes that they care about her.

Of course, any rules must be fair and reasonable. The popular phrase "tough love" does not give any adult the right to be brutal. The aim should always be discipline without dictatorship, and punishment without humiliation. When parents misuse the greater power they inevitably have through the imposition of harsh and humiliating rules and punishments, any child will feel affronted and try to get back at them. If this develops into a negative tit-for-tat pattern, the constant retaliatory put-downs will progressively erode her belief in herself.

All children thrive on the approval of both a mother and a father figure. If either of these arouses feelings of hatred and resentment instead because of harshly administered discipline or indifference, a girl will react defensively to the perceived insult and create distance between herself and the very people she needs to feel close to.

By showing you care about your daughter, by providing love and (not too many but well-chosen and consistently applied) rules, you help her to care about herself and others, including you.

37 Love her for who she is, not who you want her to be

One of the hardest things to do is to love and accept a daughter for who she is. Instead, we dwell on what we see as her flaws or focus on our dreams for her future. We worry that our hopes might be dashed. But if you focus on an idealized future, the present is likely to disappoint. And if you let your disappointment show, the relationship that should fill your daughter with confidence will only fill her with self-doubt.

While some girls are as gentle, sensitive and helpful as we are told to expect them to be, we must never forget that others will be rambunctious, energetic, sometimes clumsy and filled with an urge to explore, play and run around. We should never see these girls as "difficult." Equally, we should never take advantage of our compliant daughters, expect more from them than we would from our sons or exploit any mother–daughter intimacy that may interfere with a girl's need to become separate and independent.

Parents

- Imagine that your daughter has dropped all the characteristics that irritate you: She cleans her room, hangs up her coat, volunteers to wash up, never forgets anything. Consider whether you are left with the same girl or whether her essential personality has gone, too.
- List all of her pluses and minuses. Balance each negative characteristic with a positive one; then add more pluses than minuses to the list.
- Let her live in the present, not with your fears for the future. She has many years ahead in which to grow and mature before she's an adult.
- Be aware that if she becomes who you want her to be, she will have lost herself.

Teachers

- If a student becomes a "clone," modeling herself on you or an ideal, she is likely to find it hard to take risks and handle making mistakes.
- To help younger children appreciate who they are, outline them while they lie on paper on the floor. Then invite each child to fill in her shape with her characteristics.
- Ask older children to list twenty things they like to do, beside which they should list the date when they last did them, a $ sign beside things that cost more than $5, an "F" if they prefer to do it with a friend, an "A" if alone, a "P" if it needs planning and an "M/D" if a parent used to do it as a child. They can then tell a story about their likes and interests.

38 Don't make approval conditional on good behavior

One of the things prospective employers are wary of when they interview people for jobs is any applicant who "brown-noses," seeks approval, avoids disagreement and seems not to have faith in her own judgment. Anyone showing these tendencies is rejected because insecurity and uncertainty are unhelpful in the workplace.

Of course, we all have times when we feel unsure. However, some people suffer from insecurity more than others, and some are hindered by it most of the time.

The tendency often starts in childhood. Girls grow strong inside when they feel approved of, loved and accepted for who they are. If an adult's approval is conditional, and only forthcoming when a girl is being "good" or has done well, she will be forever looking over her shoulder, manipulating her behavior and creating distance between her instincts and her actions. Always having to play to the parental audience, she will soon lose sight of herself and be unable to develop a sense of personal integrity or confidence in herself.

Parents

- Accept that your daughter won't be perfect and that mistakes are not only inevitable but also important for learning.
- See the funny side of her errors.
- Behavior talks: She's not bad, she's just trying to say something. Look behind any bad behavior for possible reasons.
- Disapprove of what she does, not who she is.
- With older girls, you can disagree with what they want to do, yet still support their right to do it.

Teachers

- Be aware that reward systems for work and behavior might lead unsuccessful girls to feel inadequate or disapproved of.
- Show approval toward all students: Respect, show interest in and talk to each one, not just the cooperative and successful ones.
- Involve all students in decision-making, to develop their independence and self-esteem, and to demonstrate that you trust and approve of their ability to make realistic judgments.
- Value a wide range of skills.

39 Hear her complaints

When my mom picked me up from my first school, she used to stand talking with her friends for ages. I was tired, wanted her because I'd missed her and wanted to be home. Tugging at her didn't work, so one day I told her about it. She said she hadn't realized and she changed right away.

A very young child takes life as it comes, mainly because she knows no different and is in no position to pass judgment. But as her sense of self and her speech develop, she begins to reflect and see the world from her own perspective. She becomes aware of her own desires and wishes, forms her own judgments and starts seeing that things can, indeed, be different. When she puts this into words, she is expressing and risking her total experience of herself.

This is why, as soon as she is able to voice, or display, disappointment or dissatisfaction, her complaints should be taken seriously and responded to respectfully. Her self-confidence and happiness depend on it.

Parents

- Let your daughter know that it's all right to complain. Pin a sheet of paper in her bedroom for written comments if she finds it difficult to confront you.
- When you hear her complaint, it could be the first step toward compromise and an important lesson in conflict resolution.
- Hear her out: Try not to be defensive or competitive if she complains.
- Be ready to apologize if she says you have gone too far.

Teachers

- Turn any complaint into a question or statement: "It sounds like you think this grade isn't fair because you tried really hard this time, is that right?" or "I think I need to explain myself more completely. Thank you for letting me know."
- If you are able to enter a student's world, see how things are for her and accept her perspective, you will be modeling respect, empathy and emotional literacy.

40 Acknowledge her disappointments

Disappointments are part of growing up. Girls have to learn that they can't always get their way, and that when this happens, life doesn't fall apart. We have to learn to compromise, and sometimes to do without.

If parents set out to make sure that their daughter never experiences disappointment, they may end up enslaved. She will not learn to live with or overcome setbacks, and it will not help her to understand herself, because she will never have to decide which of a range of alternatives is really important to her.

However, there are times when you should not gloss over disappointments, when you should not only acknowledge them but also actively avoid them. If the people your daughter relies on and trusts let her down frequently, it can lead to a profound sadness that may later develop into a mental-health problem.

Parents

- Anticipate potential disappointments.
- Don't ignore or dismiss your daughter's sadness.
- Talk about it. Show insight and understanding by letting her know you know, and say something like, "I know you'll be disappointed, but we can't go bowling until next week," or "I know you were looking forward to that a lot. I'm sorry that it can't happen and that I raised your hopes."
- Remember that if she feels let down by you, rather than by not being allowed to have or do things, and she feels that you let her down frequently, she could begin to distance herself from you.

Teachers

- Most students are disappointed if they get a bad grade, especially if they tried hard, although they may cover up their disappointment well.
- Try to acknowledge likely feelings of disappointment when you give feedback, and if you think a student has made a special effort, acknowledge this too. Tell her not to be discouraged and assert your confidence in her ability to do better next time.
- Give her hope. Discuss with her what she thinks needs to be done and what she can do differently. End the conversation with a summary of steps she can take to improve her performance.

41 Hang on to your authority

I thought I'd lost it. She wouldn't do a thing I asked. I felt completely useless and became scared to try again in case I got ignored again. Then I realized that, just like her mother, I had all the authority I needed and I didn't need to prove it by shouting and screaming. I calmed down, thought ahead, decided on a few things I wanted her to do and stayed firm and fair. It worked, and we both feel so much better for it.

Authority can be demonstrated in many quiet ways. Adults have to find the right balance, so that they remain in charge but don't get caught up in power battles to prove it. Making firm decisions about your family's or class's routine—what you do when, or what behavior is right for your family—is one way. Being unflappable and showing trust that girls will cooperate as asked or expected is another. When you take clear responsibility for deciding things, you demonstrate your authority.

Parents

- All parents possess the authority that is ingrained in their position as a parent. You may have lost touch with your authority, but you can never lose it.
- Be aware that things such as threats and bribes, or shouting and shaming, are tools of power that children resent deeply. These actions will ultimately undermine your authority, not boost it.
- When you assume responsibility for things, you automatically acquire and display authority.
- You are the adult, so accept that responsibility. If your relationship with your daughter has been going badly, tell her she hasn't been herself, and be constant about guidelines you set.

Teachers

- If you trust a girl to behave as expected, and she in turn trusts you, this demonstrates your authority and assumes a joint responsibility for resolving the problem.
- If you make it clear from the start that your professional objective is every child's best interest, and you are able to convince students of this, when you make a mistake they will not lose faith in you or themselves.

42 Use reasons to explain, not persuade

I'm not sure why, but the more reasons I give for doing something, the more my daughter sits tight and refuses to do it.

Girls deserve to be given reasons: It shows respect for their right to know and their ability to understand. Hearing reasons teaches them how to put forward an argument and to be rational. But this approach goes wrong often, because offering more than two reasons changes what you say from an authoritative command into a much weaker exercise in persuasion.

First, children frequently switch off at the first sound of a pleading voice. They know what's coming and they feel manipulated. Second, we risk overkill by giving too many reasons. Children quickly learn that multiple reasons are a device to get them to agree, so they argue and refuse.

No more than two reasons are needed. Try saying, "This is what I want you to do and this is why; now go and do it."

Parents

- Give no more than two reasons to explain why you want something done.
- Look your daughter in the eye as you tell her, so that she can see you are serious.
- Then turn away, because this conveys the clear message that you expect her to comply. Hovering suggests that you think she won't do it, and that she will need policing.
- To avoid appearing too controlling when you want to say no, ask her to first guess what your answer and reasons are likely to be.

Teachers

- If a student asks for something outside the accepted rules, ask her to repeat the rule and anticipate what your answer is going to be. She then arrives at the answer "no" without you coming across as negative.
- Give no more than two reasons to explain why a student has to do something.

43 Be fun, fair and flexible

My granddad grew up in a mining town where all the families had strict rules. But for one day, once a year, all those rules were dropped. The children were allowed to do what they wanted: knock on elderly neighbors' doors and generally go wild. They let off steam and everyone had fun. It sounded great!

While many girls seem to enjoy the safety and security offered by structure, none will thrive if she feels she is in the grip of an unrelenting disciplinarian.

Girls give their respect and full cooperation only if the rules are clear but remain in the background, and if their daily experience is characterized by fun, fairness and enough flexibility for them to feel they are listened to, loved and treated as individuals.

Parents

- Make time for family fun, activities and games with your daughter.
- Hiding birthday and other annual presents or chocolates around the house as a treasure hunt adds to the fun and shows you have made an effort to do something special for her.
- All children love family rituals, which can happen weekly, monthly or annually. If these can be fun, involving some relaxation of rules such as a scheduled bedtime, girls will enjoy them even more.
- Flexibility, backed by a reason and agreed on with a twinkle in your eye, won't lead to any loss of authority—insensitive rigidity will.

Teachers

- Curriculum planning and goals offer little scope for flexibility, but you can introduce fun into lessons through educational quizzes and games.
- Try to see mild pranks played on you as girls having fun and letting off steam. If you let these annoy or upset you, they'll target you again.
- Be creative: Adapt a lesson to address an issue currently making the headlines or make the lesson relevant to your students' everyday lives.
- Being fair means not just treating all students equally but also being sensitive to the reasons behind their behavior.

44 Rules reduce conflict

Discipline is the aspect of parenting that causes most parents the most heartache. It is also the thing most parents feel they do not get right. This isn't surprising because there is rarely a "right" answer: The rules have to shift as children grow and circumstances change.

Creating family rules is difficult because it involves balancing different people's needs and demands, managing different and developing personalities and sometimes compromising between different cultures and values.

Family rules that are mutually agreed upon and clearly understood undoubtedly reduce conflict. It's conflict that does the harm, not the rules. Clear expectations and well-established, consistent daily patterns for you and your daughter reduce the number of challenges. When she sees that you mean business, your daughter will stop testing you.

Parents

- Conflict isn't avoided in the long term by giving in. Your daughter will only learn that the more she pushes, the more often she will get her own way.
- All children like the security that rules provide.
- Being rule-abiding at home will help girls to be law-abiding later.
- If you feel you are losing control, prioritize: Stand firm on the issues you care most about and drop the rest.

Teachers

- Clearly stated rules applied fairly and consistently throughout the school by all staff help children to know where they stand and to feel secure.
- Involve the girls themselves whenever possible in agreeing on the rules so that they learn to take responsibility and don't feel dictated to.
- Have explicit, gradated consequences for well-defined breaches of the rules.

45 Avoid wielding the tools of power

When I was a teenager, my mother was terrified I would get pregnant. She told me that if it ever happened, I would be out in the street. I was really hurt. How could she do that to me? After a huge argument one day, I considered the best way to get back at her. I almost went out to have unprotected sex just to spite her.

The tools of power that adults are inclined to use are hitting, hurting, damaging children's belongings, bribery, ridicule, threats, sarcasm, shouting, emotional withdrawal and withholding food and freedom. It may be tempting to use these sometimes, especially when your patience is thin, but it will be counterproductive. Your daughter will simply find a way to get back at you to preserve her self-respect.

Children deserve the best from their parents, not the worst.

Parents

• It is best not to force an issue when either you or your child is tired. Let it go, in case it blows up in both your faces.

• Try using the "soft no": If your daughter does not respond the first time you ask her to do something, instead of raising your voice and issuing threats, repeat your request more quietly, making sure that you and she are looking directly at each other.

• Try trusting her to comply, giving one or two reasons, or using creative ways to get compliance (without bribery).

Teachers

• Responding with instant punishments in an apparently arbitrary way is an abuse of power. Be measured, fair and consistent to avoid resentment and maintain students' cooperation.

• Avoid using sarcasm and ridicule in the classroom. These are not appropriate tools for any professional.

• Don't take challenges personally. They may not be intended as such and you run the risk of a communication breakdown.

• People usually shout and throw things when their patience and skills are exhausted. Consider team-teaching to refresh your skills if you lose control more than occasionally.

46 As the adult, it's your job to repair

My daughter and I couldn't see eye to eye. We had one bad patch when we didn't speak for nine months.

When your relationship with your daughter breaks, however much you think she is at fault, it's your job as the adult to mend it. You have the greater wisdom, maturity, confidence and skill to achieve this. Refusing to acknowledge or communicate with your daughter is no way to teach her how to repair a relationship or to give her confidence in herself.

Parents

• When your daughter's behavior is awful, try not to take it personally. Often she will act like that to get attention or to protect herself, not to get at you, unless she feels she has good cause. It is unnecessary to retaliate.

• You don't have to win every battle. Take responsibility for the bad patch and make the first overture toward peace.

• Make the second, third and fourth moves. Trust is thin after a bad patch, so don't expect any immediate change. Making up should not depend on immediate reciprocation.

Teachers

• Personality clashes between students and teachers happen. If one seems to rub you the wrong way, it's your responsibility to work it out. Be open with the student, reflect on any past personal experiences that may explain your reactions, and take responsibility. Arranging for her to work with a different teacher may be the only way out.

• Be aware that personal and professional stress can undermine skills and tolerance. If stress is affecting you, be open about your state of mind, apologize, state your needs clearly and your class will almost certainly offer cooperation and understanding.

47 Discipline without dictatorship

All girls need boundaries and a framework of rules to help them control and manage their behavior and fit into their family or school. Boundaries and rules help keep girls safe and acceptable to others. They also allow adults to show that they care about what happens to the girls and also to become involved in their world.

Reasonable rules and self-esteem go hand in hand. Clear boundaries make a child's world structured, planned, predictable and safe. They give it a rhythm and pattern. But this is achieved only when family discipline acknowledges and respects the needs and rights of the child. Discipline that is inflexible and that strives to humiliate will, steadily and inevitably, chip away at a girl's self-confidence.

Parents

- Be clear: Prioritize, don't have too many rules, and keep them simple.
- Be firm, but also friendly and loving. Stick to your rules 90 percent of the time, but be flexible when it really matters to your daughter.
- Be fair, because this is the best way to keep her from becoming resentful.
- Be consistent: Try to respond in the same way each time and get your partner to do the same.
- Keep your love constant: Don't blow hot and cold.
- Set a good example: Behave as you expect your daughter to behave.

Teachers

- Dictatorship no longer works in the classroom, if it ever did. Military-style orders and insults are unacceptable.
- As with parents, be clear, be firm, be fair, be consistent, be fun and be flexible, giving reasons whenever you adapt or relax the rules.
- Plan for variety and use different teaching styles to engage all students naturally.
- Ban threats, sarcasm, insults, ridicule and shouting from your repertoire.

48 Punishment without humiliation

My dad used to make me sit at the dinner table with no clothes on when I'd been "bad." And he thought he was justified because he hadn't laid a finger on me. I've hated him ever since.

There are effective and ineffective ways to show girls how to manage their behavior. The use of punishments that humiliate is ineffective in the long term because they make children resentful. Though they may do as they are told at the time, their obedience is the result of force. This won't lead to future cooperation.

For children to learn effective lessons from punishment, it should focus on what they have done wrong and not cause resentment, anger, bitterness or other bad feelings. In other words, it should be fair and leave a child's self-respect intact. If you put her down, there will be repercussions. Being frequently subjected to humiliating punishments will eventually cause a child to feel shame, guilt, self-doubt and ultimately self-hate, and it may lead to anger, hostility and destructive and self-destructive behavior.

Parents

- If you use punishments, try to be clear, fair, consistent and sensitive to their effect. Keep them brief and show your daughter soon afterward that you still love her.
- Deal with only one behavior at a time. Don't pile on the complaints or punishments.
- Punish the act and not the person.
- Alternatives to physical punishment include withdrawal of privileges; restricted use of a favorite toy or pastime; withdrawal of allowance; being sent to a cooling-off place; a verbal telling-off; and an early bedtime.

Teachers

- Always give fair warning of any punishment you might give.
- Make sure your behavior policy contains clear and gradated consequences for clearly defined behavior.
- If students challenge you and fake indifference, don't up the ante and impose harsher punishments.
- Ensure the punishment fits, and is relevant to, the crime.
- Avoid taking challenges personally, because when that happens, the punishment may become personal, too.

49 Model effective conflict resolution

Constant conflict ruins relationships and tears families apart. Children are deeply scarred by conflict, particularly when it becomes physical and takes place between their parents. Family conflict lies behind much teenage despair that is expressed through depression and self-destructive behavior.

But we can't get rid of all conflict. Different people inevitably have different and conflicting views and interests that have to be reconciled. Also, each of us has times when we feel exposed and vulnerable, when we are inclined to see comments and actions as challenges. We take these personally, and react aggressively, even when no challenge was intended. What we can do is understand why and when this happens and learn how to manage and resolve it when it does, so that it does not get out of hand.

Resolving conflict safely and satisfactorily takes emotional maturity and social skill. Children have to be taught successful attitudes and approaches by the adults who care for them.

Parents

• Good communication skills are the basis for successful conflict management. Listen to your daughter's case, present yours using only "I" statements, not provocative "You" statements, and seek a compromise.

• Acknowledge the feelings as well as the different interests that underlie the dispute.

•You don't need to win every battle. Sidestep the issue if it isn't critical and avoid arguments when either you or your daughter is tired.

• Friction between siblings teaches about conflict. If older ones can be left together safely, let them figure out their problem in their own time; younger ones may need help.

Teachers

• All schools should adopt a clear policy of nonviolence.

• A table can be set aside for children who have begun to argue to discuss their differences safely.

• All school staff, including cafeteria and playground supervisors, can be briefed about nonviolent ways to resolve conflicts.

• Personal and social education programs should contain lessons on violence prevention and effective strategies to manage and resolve conflict.

• How you respond to challenges in class sets a strong example.

CHAPTER 6

Responding Sensitively to Setbacks

Life presents everyone, including children, with experiences that can knock them for a loop. It is part of every school's and caregiver's job to prepare the girls they take care of for these troublesome times. Being bullied or excluded from groups, families breaking up, friendships ending, bereavement or separations, and disappointments at school or on the sports field are common experiences. Children can't be protected from every possible hurt, however much parents may wish to and however desirable this is—and it may not be. But how can adults help to rebuild a girl's self-esteem when all she wants to do is run away and hide?

Most of us know a child who seems to be made of rubber and wears a permanent grin. Nothing seems to get her down. Whatever the problem, she has the ability to take the knocks, keep her attention fixed on a better future, and make her way steadily, knowingly and confidently toward it. Such a girl is called *resilient.* She lives with and through problems, gets herself back on course, can move on and even use setbacks to strengthen and enrich herself.

Recovery from troubles is more likely when adults

respond sensitively to a girl's setbacks. When they manage her confusion and dejection well, she retains self-respect and self-esteem to face the world again and treat the obstacle as an opportunity to grow and learn.

Resilience is sometimes described as the ability to bounce back; however, this misrepresents what happens. Staying power involves action, not reaction. People with stamina and persistence think, feel, perceive and understand themselves and their situation in a way that enables them to remain positive, active and able to recognize the lessons to be learned. Resilient girls overcome problems and recover from obstacles by using a variety of skills, attributes and strategies, often helped by adults.

What gives girls staying power? Recent studies of children who recover from setbacks show that personality plays a small part, but more helpful factors are a tendency to see themselves in a good light, having at least one good, close relationship with an adult, and not being exposed to too many problems.

Girls who bounce back have a good sense of their own worth and abilities, believe they can shape what happens to them, are good at solving problems, mix happily with others, maintain friendships and are generally optimistic about life. Parents and teachers can help girls by encouraging this and by responding sensitively to them.

50 Give her safe time to talk

After my parents split up, I stayed with my dad every other weekend. The only time he asked me how I was doing was during the short trip home in the car. He wasn't really interested. He was making it safe for him to talk, not for me.

When girls feel close to someone and are able to make sense of whatever has happened to them, they are more likely to recover from setbacks. Talking usually helps, but the time and place to talk has to be right. There's no point in raising the issue in a place where the conversation will be overheard, where either of you feel uncomfortable, or when there's insufficient time to explore and come to some conclusion, even if this means saying, "We need more time to talk."

This is particularly true if your daughter is ashamed about the event or if she feels responsible—if she has been bullied at school or been found cheating or stealing, for example. Children sometimes feel guilty about problems for which their parents are responsible, such as the breakdown of a marriage. Even if they don't truly believe they're to blame, they may still feel that they should have prevented what happened.

Parents

- Avoid being intrusive. Before you talk, check that your daughter's ready.
- Make sure that there is enough time to talk before you begin.
- Make it clear from the start that the conversation is confidential.
- If you want to pass along any of it, get her permission: "Do you mind if I tell Dad/Mom/your teacher what you've said?"
- If she finds it hard to talk, suggest going for a walk together. Tell her you are ready to talk when she is, but let her take the initiative.
- Girls sometimes prefer to figure things out in their own heads rather than talk. Be aware this can be equally successful for solving the issue.

Teachers

- Buddy or mentor programs are useful in the upper grade school and middle school years and enable pupils to talk to their peers.
- In the early middle school years, teachers play a vital role. They should be selected for their proven abilities in dealing sensitively with students.
- Any references to personal issues or problems in students' work should be taken seriously and responded to sensitively, not ignored.

51 Fortify her heart, don't thicken her skin

Many parents believe the best way to arm their daughters against verbal attack and disappointment is to thicken their skin, to get them to "toughen up." They achieve this in two ways: Some dish out hurtful words and crush expectations just to get a girl used to it, to create an immunity to pain. Others constantly tell their daughter that she should not be feeling the way she does, that her emotions make her vulnerable to the harshness of life and to other people. They tell her to deny or repress her feelings.

A far better way to protect her is to strengthen her inside—her heart and her self-belief—not outside. Trying to toughen her outer shell not only does great damage to a girl's self-confidence and self-understanding, it also cuts her off from her essential self in the process. Suits of emotional armor stop feelings from coming out as well as going in, so they offer no long-term help with managing relationships.

Parents

• Build up your daughter's inner strength: Trust her; see her as competent; let her have some autonomy in her life; tell her you love her; and respect her view of the world.

• If she's in trouble, understand her feelings, support her and help her through. Don't put her down by saying, "Why did you let yourself get into this mess?"

• Encourage her to follow and trust her instincts: *Encourage* means to give her courage.

• Give her assertive words, phrases and actions to use when she feels threatened, such as, "I don't know why you need to say/do these things that hurt others" and "I don't have to listen to you" and turn away. Discuss which ones she'll be happy to use.

Teachers

• Constantly monitor the different ways in which you talk to girls and boys.

• Don't fall victim to expressing stereotypical views about either girls or boys.

52 Nurture her self-respect

When things go wrong for your daughter, she is likely to feel embarrassed or even humiliated. She may think that she has let either you or herself down, which may make her feel anxious if you are generally intolerant of her making mistakes. It is natural and quite common for children to keep problems, such as being bullied, to themselves. Especially if and when her problem becomes public knowledge, your daughter may be ashamed of the position in which she finds herself. Her self-respect will have been damaged, even if she is not really to blame.

In order to pick herself up and face the world again, what she needs most is a double dose of self-belief and self-respect. However you feel about what has happened, your prime role must be to help repair the damage that was done and to leave your daughter with enough self-respect to try again. Humiliating her won't work.

Parents

• Your daughter will learn to respect herself if she sees that you respect her.

• Those who are frequently blamed and shamed will find it hard to hold on to their self-respect, but they can retain it and redeem their mistakes if they are guided sensitively, without criticism or insult.

• Self-respect grows in part from the experience of being given responsibilities and carrying them out successfully.

• Children shirk responsibility and will not learn self-respect if they are allowed to ignore any painful consequences of their choices or behavior.

Teachers

• Show respect for your students, so that they can respect themselves.

• Help them to see the good in themselves and in what they achieve.

• Independent learning helps students learn to trust and respect their own judgment and not to hold back out of fear of failure.

• Encourage pupils to respect each other, to listen respectfully and share successes. In small groups, ask them to share a success, accomplishment or achievement they had between certain ages—before they were ten, between ten and twelve and so on—as is appropriate to the group.

53 Avoid shame and guilt

Shame and guilt are natural human feelings. When people have specific duties and responsibilities, and they fall short of meeting them, it is natural that they feel some shame or guilt. So why is it so important for a girl's self-esteem to protect her from too much shame?

Shame and guilt are difficult and destructive emotions for all children. They create doubt and confusion. The child has let herself or someone else down and probably doesn't understand why or how. Sometimes it is appropriate for a girl to feel shame or guilt: for example, if she's old enough to be clear about what she should be doing and can manage her behavior and be held fully responsible for it—if these feelings come from within herself. Punishing your daughter by making her feel ashamed and guilty won't work. Instead of changing her ways, she is more likely to suppress the uncomfortable guilt feelings and deny any responsibility for the problem.

Parents

• Make it clear to your daughter that any relationship or marital breakdown you are suffering is not her fault.

• Even if she has tried to sabotage a new relationship of yours, focus on what worries her about the change rather than blaming her.

• Concentrate on addressing the practical consequences of her difficult behavior. Your shame or embarrassment are your problem, not hers.

• If she is being bullied, talk about what she might do to prevent it, and inform her school. Don't tell her she is weak.

• It's for her to decide how she feels about her mistakes, and for you to decide the consequences.

Teachers

• Instead of rubbing a girl's nose in her errors, make your expectations clear.

• It's all right for a student to feel guilt or shame spontaneously. It is not all right for you to make her feel guilty or ashamed.

• Sarcasm, ridicule and teasing rarely spur children to greater effort, because the shame they cause undermines confidence.

• Don't punish the whole class for something only a few have done. It arouses widespread resentment, not repentance in the guilty ones.

• Don't blame students for something for which you are responsible.

54 Offer extra closeness

When a girl experiences stress and problems, she will need the reassurance of the adults she depends on even more. Yet if parents feel any anger or disappointment, they are more likely to withdraw than to draw closer. Children understand themselves through their key relationships—those they have with friends, family and caring professionals. If these supports disappear in her time of need, a girl will doubt herself even more profoundly.

Not only will she lose confidence in herself and question her identity, she will be further confused and unsettled by the altered behavior of those she relies upon.

All changes are stressful for children. In times of change and stress, try to stay close to your daughter and be available to her more.

Parents

- Changes that may upset your daughter can include moving; starting a new school; illness in the family; bereavement; a new relationship of yours or problems in your current one.
- Depending on your daughter's age, you can be close to her by staying with her while she bathes; sitting on her bed at night; sitting next to her while she watches TV; keeping her company as she walks to the bus stop; giving her lifts in the car and chatting as you drive.

Teachers

- Spend time with younger girls in the quiet corner.
- Ask students to help you with tasks.
- Find time for little personal conversations.
- Constantly offer yourself as someone with whom a student may "talk things through" or suggest other people who could do the same (friends, parents, another teacher or a peer mentor, for example).

55 Help her see the lessons to be learned

Don't despair; start to repair! Parents and teachers offer effective help when they remain nonjudgmental and let a girl figure out for herself what went wrong or what she did wrong, and how she can move forward again in a practical and confident way. There is always something to be learned from setbacks. Rather than playing the victim and blaming someone else, your daughter has the option to come through difficult experiences stronger, wiser and more competent.

Stay positive. Instead of asking, "What will you avoid doing next time?" you can ask, "What might you do differently next time?"

Not all setbacks will fit this model. If a child is feeling down because she has been bullied, had a quarrel on the playground or been dumped by a boyfriend, she will not necessarily have done anything wrong. But there will still be conclusions to draw and the solution should come from her. Problems are best reflected and acted upon, not recoiled from or smoothed away by an overprotective parent.

Parents

- Unravel and break down the problem. If something went wrong, there will be practical reasons why.
- Don't let your daughter tell herself that she's "useless" or that she'll "never be any good." Setbacks should not be seen as unalterable omens of her future, but as learning opportunities.
- Ask her what she thinks went wrong. Don't tell her what you think unless she asks or says she's happy to listen.
- Identifying the lessons to be learned is energizing. When she can see what went wrong, she will know how to correct it and regain control.

Teachers

- Making a student aware of the control she has over her daily life enhances her self-concept. Ensure that organizational devices such as calendars and homework schedules are used regularly and effectively.
- We find out about ourselves through taking responsibility. Coping with the consequences of our mistakes provides such an opportunity.
- Encourage students to develop the habit of asking the questions, "What are the lessons to be learned?" and "What have I learned?" They both foster reflection.
- If a student fails to do her homework, ask for a realistic plan for making up the lost ground.

56 Hear her side of the story

When a girl has a setback, depending on the nature of the problem, it is common for parents either to take it personally and feel shamed by it or to see the problem as a nonissue. This can encourage them to belittle their daughter's fears and concerns. If you have heard only the bare facts of the case, do not assume that your daughter is at fault, or tell her off for putting you in a difficult position with, for example, neighbors, the police or the school.

If she is upset about something you consider minor, try to see the issue from her point of view. Adults and children perceive things differently, so avoid applying your judgments unthinkingly. Saying things like "Stop making it such a big deal," "It will pass," and "I can't understand why you're bothered by that" won't help your daughter resolve her problem. Encouraging her to think it through will.

Hearing her side of the story shows that you respect her and want to treat her fairly and seriously. It will help to maintain her self-confidence.

Parents

- Let your daughter tell you about her disappointments, and don't belittle them.
- Assume the best of her, not the worst.
- In arguments between brothers and sisters, hear each one out, then ask them in turn what they see as a possible solution.
- A child doesn't always want you to solve her problems. She may just want to talk things through and be listened to. Keep your opinions to yourself.

Teachers

- Don't assume a student is in the wrong if she has a grievance against a teacher. Suggest she go to the principal or school counselor to state her case, somewhere neutral where she will be listened to and taken seriously.
- Avoid making quick, prejudiced judgments. Just because a girl has a reputation for being troublesome does not mean she is implicated in every problem. Hear her side of the story.

57 Identify the danger times and signs

When Debbie was twelve, her parents separated and her world collapsed. When she returned from a week off school, she had trouble keeping up with deadlines, maintaining standards and doing homework. She started to break down over little things. It took her about a year to catch up, and three years later she was still vulnerable to any kind of setback.

Children's resilience inevitably lessens when their parents or caregivers split up, and during bereavements and other forms of family upheaval. They are also particularly vulnerable when they start or change schools. Most parents appreciate that children may be unnerved when they enter middle school or high school, but even moving from preschool to an adjacent grade school can be stressful.

Girls' confidence is fragile when they pass through key developmental stages, too: at the age of about eight and at the onset of puberty and adolescence. At these times, girls need plenty of attention.

Parents

• Your daughter will need a lot of support and attention when she starts middle school (or junior high) and for the following two years.

• Situations that can destabilize children include

- domestic violence
- racial abuse and harassment
- constant criticism and abuse
- multiple home/school moves
- divorce and separation
- bullying
- family reformation
- bereavements
- temporary absence of a parent
- illness/disability in the family

Teachers

• Signs that children are in emotional trouble include being

- withdrawn, alone, lonely, sad, prone to tears, tired and inclined to fall asleep
- unable to concentrate
- reluctant to attempt work
- aloof and rejecting help
- unable to follow classroom routines
- needy or contriving helplessness in order to get constant reassurance
- likely to destroy their own or other children's work
- afraid to mix with others
- aggressive, spacy or dependent
- the class clown
- a frequent target for bullying
- a liar, thief or cheat
- late often
- absent frequently

58 Dealing sensitively with peer pressure

Peer pressure, along with bullying and drugs, is a subject that frightens many parents. We like to believe that our daughters will be sufficiently independent to withstand the pull of her peer group, especially when the group's activities are dangerous or illegal.

Children generally love to conform and hate to be different. Their earliest flirtation with self-expression and independence from parents is frequently by the safe route of fashion, and the younger they are when they make choices about clothes, hairstyles or how they spend their time, the more likely it is that fashion will be the route they choose. Keep in mind: Not all peer groups are up to no good.

Parents

- Don't drive your daughter into the arms of antisocial friends by being constantly critical. The best way to help her resist negative peer pressure is to nurture her self-esteem and give her inner strength.
- If she wants expensive clothes or money to go out, ask that she contributes something toward it, and make this possible with a regular allowance or part-time wages if she's old enough.
- Ask her for her definition of a friend and question whether people who won't allow her to be different are truly friends.
- Remember, girls who are vulnerable to peer pressure are impressionable. Help your daughter feel acceptable as she is.

Teachers

- Be aware of the power of peer groups to divert some girls from their studies. A peer mentorship program can offer vulnerable girls a listening ear.
- Discuss the issue of peer pressure in assembly, physical education classes, health classes and any other relevant setting.
- Many girls who are seduced away from learning are vulnerable because they are already failing. Identify those who may be at risk as early as possible and offer them after-school help in order to keep them on track.

59 Keep her informed of developments

One of the most important needs we all have is to be kept informed about changes and events that affect us. We get annoyed if employers, partners, the local government or neighbors do things that affect us without letting us know in advance. Children need to be told things, too, especially if their families are experiencing changes.

If you and your partner are having a trial or permanent separation or are going through a divorce; if someone in the family is ill and needs a lot of medication or has to go to the hospital, perhaps for an operation; or if you are looking for a new school for her, your daughter will want to know how things stand. All children can be panicked into thinking the worst or disappointed by an unrealistic dream if they have only sketchy information to go on.

As stated earlier, if you keep your daughter informed, then you show respect for her right to know, for her need to understand what's happening to her and for her ability to take in that information and use it sensibly.

Parents

- Children should be kept informed about events and changes (before, during and after they happen), feelings (yours and theirs), decisions and facts.
- Anyone who feels uncomfortable discussing issues such as going into the hospital, dying, divorce or moving may prefer to raise the matter using a children's book that explores the subject through a combination of story and factual information.
- Children need to make sense of their world and what is happening to them. Keeping them informed of developments is an important way to do this.

Teachers

- Ensure that students know exactly why something is happening, from the very basic, such as what the goals of a particular lesson are, to why a student is being moved to a different group, who will teach the class while you are away and so on.

60 Find good support groups

When my mom died, my life fell apart. My friends at school and the swim team were the two things that kept me going. The team got me out of the house and made me feel normal. My friends were just great.

Research into what helps children and young people manage difficult personal events shows that they do better when they are involved in a range of groups and feel part of a wider community.

Belonging to a group can help girls feel secure about who they are at a time when they might question their identity. It is reassuring because their commitments maintain normal daily and weekly patterns and routines. It also enables them to receive the understanding and support of people who know them and have time for them.

Parents

- Help your daughter attend her regular groups and clubs during troubled times.
- If she has few commitments outside school, see if she can become involved in other activities locally.
- If she's having problems at school, out-of-school groups can help her start new relationships with a clean slate.
- If you think she's mixing with the wrong group of friends, keep an eye on her.
- Don't let your need for her company isolate her from her friends.

Teachers

- Encourage vulnerable girls to sign up for lunchtime clubs and after-school activities where they can develop friendships and new skills and rebuild their confidence.
- Vulnerable girls may benefit from being kept together in stable class groups, which offer security and support.

61 Minimize conflicts at home

This is a hard one, because arguments are a natural part of family life. However, it is disturbing for girls when home is characterized by conflict in their eyes. And it is clear that domestic violence and conflict are associated with girls who have particularly low self-esteem.

Conflict is unsettling. When girls are going through a difficult time, and already feel stressed, parents should take extra care to avoid arguments, both between themselves and with the girl concerned. When parents fight, verbally or physically, their daughters can feel pressure to take sides, which splits them down the middle.

How can parents know when their family conflict is greater than "normal"? Features that probably make a difference include frequency (obviously); who is involved; what the disagreement is about; whether it becomes noisy or personalized; whether verbal or physical violence, abuse or bullying are involved; and whether and how the conflict is resolved.

Parents

- Consider banning arguments during difficult times.
- Encourage everyone in the family to write down their complaints instead. These can be discussed at a set time, say, once a week.
- Remember that personal insults, shouting and abuse will damage your daughter's self-esteem.
- Discussion and debate are healthy and are not the same as conflict.
- Teaching and modeling ways to resolve conflict will be of lifelong benefit to your daughter.

Teachers

- Conflict at home can affect girls' schoolwork, especially when it is serious enough to be described as domestic violence. The school must take it seriously.
- Discussions about conflict at home and at school, why it happens and different ways to resolve it should be part of all students' personal and social education program.
- If girls hear that others experience the same problems, it may help them to cope.

CHAPTER 7

Supporting Her Learning and Personal Growth

Children do well when their parents are openly interested in what they do and support them, and when they have a strong, realistic sense of themselves and what they can achieve. "I believe I can do it" is as important as "I want to do it." Both are far more important for long-term achievement than "I was made to do it."

Given that the key to successful learning and personal development is self-motivation, what can parents and teachers do to encourage this? From research undertaken in the business world, we know that the best motivators are people who try to see merit in an idea even when it is different from their own; accept mistakes if lessons are learned; are easy to talk to, even when under pressure; have consistent high yet realistic expectations; encourage people to develop themselves and give credit when credit is due. From sports psychology, we know that the best coaches focus on improving technique and skill, not on the goal of winning, and discourage athletes from judging themselves by results. They make rewards reflect achievements; teach individuals to handle their own mistakes, learning and progress; and reduce anxiety by finding out what is causing it and addressing that directly.

Learning and growing inevitably involve change and

taking risks, the unpleasant possibility of outright failure, confronting personal limitations, and the excitement of potential discoveries. When girls feel competent and good about themselves, they are likely to be positive about their present and future skills and talents. Confident girls are happy to change.

Girls who feel unsure of who they are will feel pessimistic about what they are capable of achieving. But they will often avoid acknowledging this, and sidestep failure and change by claiming they know it all already or have no need to know. Seeing learning as irrelevant to one's future is simply one further, highly convenient and seemingly respectable way of avoiding taking responsibility for success and failure.

Girls who fail to master the basic skills at school may eventually stop trying to achieve anything. Instead, they may focus on what remains within their power to control and give: their body and their sexuality. Helping girls to grow in confidence and explore their practical and intellectual talents requires supporting their schoolwork and giving them reason to consider themselves worthy of effort.

But when girls are depressed, anxious or angry, when they feel let down by adults or are preoccupied with any problem, they cannot concentrate on their work. During these times, try to maintain routines and offer as much emotional support as possible.

62 Encourage and value a range of skills

As a young girl, I followed my father around the house when he was fixing things. I loved to see how things worked and I learned a lot. When I set up my own home, I saved lots of money by doing some big jobs myself.

Every girl will have many talents. She may be good at soccer, dancing, drawing, constructing paper models, cooking, climbing trees, rollerblading or ice skating. She may be knowledgeable about insects, animals, dinosaurs, gardening or pop music. Or she may be best at thinking things through or organizing herself and others. Perhaps she is quick to understand how someone else feels.

Children do best when they are well informed about or successful at something, and when they enjoy a range of activities. It is a parent's job to identify and value the various talents and skills their daughter possesses and draw her attention to them. Academic prowess should never be the sole criterion used to evaluate a child.

Parents

• Try to broaden your daughter's base of achievement: Let her sample a range of activities and skills from those that are available locally.

• Every child will benefit from believing she is good at something, such as doing puzzles, playing with other children, being creative with color and paints, or working with computers.

• Keep television-watching in check: Your daughter needs balance and variety to get the best from herself.

• Involve her in some way in the practical do-it-yourself and everyday tasks you do around your home.

Teachers

• Find something that each student is good at, tell each one what she does well, then work to develop her strengths and interests.

• If a girl has an unusual talent, encourage the other children to respect her skill, but first discover it yourself!

• Work hard to break down gender-stereotypical choices in projects and activities.

• Set up after-school and between-class clubs to introduce students to new interests.

63 Support and encourage, don't control and push

Support and encouragement will give your daughter the energy to go that extra mile when she's struggling. But support and encouragement can easily turn into controlling and pushing, which often backfires, leaving an exhausted and resentful child who may opt out of success.

The words themselves suggest when the line may be crossed. "Support" implies sharing the strain or burden. "Encourage" means to give confidence, to help someone to be brave about doing something new or difficult. By contrast, adults who control and push girls don't share their burdens, they add to them. They imply that a girl cannot be trusted to handle something on her own. The expectations and goals they set are more likely to undermine her belief in herself and sap her courage than to build it up.

Parents who control and push tend to finish tasks for their daughter; commit her to too many extracurricular activities; point out mistakes immediately; use threats and bribes; set new goals in quick succession; complain to the school often; hover and get involved in her homework, even correcting mistakes she makes.

Parents

- Take an interest in your daughter's hobbies and pastimes. Watch her doing them (without hovering) and ask how things went, especially when she made a special effort.
- Offer to take her where she needs to go and discuss any problems she has. Try to answer her questions.
- Listen to what she tells you and share her excitement about her ambitions and dreams.
- Trust her to set her own goals in a time-frame she can manage, and let her work using her own preferred learning style and work patterns.
- Remember: Children are people, not puppets or performers. If you control, push and pull, their life can become an act.

Teachers

- Give each student detailed information about the progress she's made and what she still needs to do.
- Help her to devise a plan of action if she gets stuck, to keep her on track.
- Be enthusiastic about her improvements.
- Use stars and incentives carefully, because they can be manipulative. If a girl decides not to cooperate, she may be left with nothing to work for.
- Letters, postcards, or certificates sent directly to a girl's home allow parents to be enthusiastic about recognized achievements.

64 Trust that she'll manage

I sit with her every night when she does her homework, and then I check it. If it's not right, I make her do it over again.

A fundamental, unspoken and mutual trust is created between mother and infant at birth. At that moment, the infant must trust that her mother will care and provide for her, and the mother trusts, in turn, that the infant will love and need her. As your daughter grows older, if you do not trust her, it insults her. Growing up involves facing new situations and experiences at a rate most adults would find enormously stressful. It takes great courage to do this. Your daughter needs to believe in herself to cope with new things confidently. Imagine the hurt, and the devastating blow to her pride, if the person whose opinion she most trusts assumes that she will fail—often before she has really tried.

Parents

- Trust your daughter's competence, her ability to see a task through, her judgment, her responsibility and her capacity to trust and praise her ideas.
- When she's attempting something, tell her you believe she can do it. Walk away. Don't hover over her expecting problems, or say, "Can I help?"
- Balancing a part-time job and schoolwork is possible with careful time management. Let her try it before you ban it.
- If she starts a new school, trust that she'll cope. Saying, "I hope you will/will not . . ." suggests that you fear the opposite.
- If she's finished studying, don't push her do just a little more.

Teachers

- Ask a student if she thinks she can handle something. If she says yes, affirm her self-belief.
- Occasionally, work presented as a challenge does get results. A girl will strive harder if told, "Now I'm not sure you can handle this." However, use this tactic sparingly during adolescence, when girls' self-confidence is fragile. Only use it when you firmly believe a student can deliver and is unlikely to view the challenge as a personal slight.

65 Make it safe to make mistakes

Your daughter will need tons of self-belief to make the most of her potential, but she won't have this if you criticize her every time she makes a mistake.

Mistakes are an essential part of learning. "Everyone gets scars on the way to the stars," wrote the songwriter Fran Landesman. Mistakes are also useful because they shed light on the task at hand. They show what does and does not work, and what needs to be done differently. Mistakes tell a story, and it is the story we need to understand.

Companies now understand this. The motto of one national technology company is, "If everything you do is a success, then you have failed," because mistakes show that someone has the confidence to take risks and be creative. Business today rewards employees for managing errors rather than punishing people for making them.

If you fear and deny your own mistakes, you won't help your daughter. Love her for who she is, mistakes and all, not only when she is perfect.

Parents

- Be honest and lighthearted about your own mistakes, and point out what you have learned.
- Give your daughter time to notice her own errors, or say, for example, "I see two problems here, can you?"
- Careless homework could suggest she's not doing it in the best place, at the best time, or in the best way. Seek her views.
- If she lets herself down under the pressure of exams, she might be investing too much in her results or worrying about your reaction to them.
- Unexpected mistakes could mean that she has misunderstood something, hasn't done enough work, hasn't used the right method or is worried.

Teachers

- Be honest about your mistakes: State what you've learned and apologize for them if relevant.
- If a particular girl is more careless than usual, it could be because of your teaching method. Or she may be distracted, upset, or anxious about making errors.
- Raise the class's awareness of their attitude toward making mistakes by encouraging discussion. Note whether the girls react differently than the boys.
- Unlike boys, girls (in general) prefer clearly defined tasks that do not entail risks, but risk-taking is something they need to get used to. Give them open-ended, risk-focused work, and reflect as a class on their reactions to it.

66 Have realistic expectations

My six-year-old daughter's report card was positive about every aspect of her work and social development. When I said, "Good job," she turned away and muttered, "It was a stupid report. What's the point of telling me I'm good when it's so easy?"

People perform according to expectation. They tend to live up to—or down to—their reputations. Too many children fail for too long simply because they are not asked to do any better. They never realize what they could achieve because they never stretch themselves, and they believe the limits of their capability to be those implied by the easy goals they set.

However, parents and teachers have had it so drummed into them that they must raise their expectations, we are now in danger of going too far the other way. A goal set too high is as unhelpful as one set too low. Challenges must tempt, not intimidate, deter or exhaust. Goals that are too high can lead to failure, shake your daughter's confidence and make her believe that succeeding is the only way to gain your approval.

Parents

- Ask your daughter what she thinks she can handle.
- Help her make clear plans for meeting her goal.
- Invite her to think ahead about any problems she might meet and how she'll manage any setbacks.
- Invite her to select short-term goals, which seem more achievable, as well as long-term ones.

Teachers

- Make sure the goal, time and quality of conditions for the work you set are clear, and let your students assess whether they have met the conditions.
- Encourage planning and reflective skills.
- Ask for a detailed study plan if you detect overconfidence. Don't tell a student that her goal is unreachable.
- Ask students whether they're ready for the next challenge or want time to let their new achievements sink in.
- Be clear, practical and realistic about your own goals.

67 Read and learn together

Technology has simplified our lives so we no longer lead simple lives.

—Trond Waage,
Norway's Ombudsman for Children

So close your laptop to free up your lap for your child.

Girls are known to develop speech and language ahead of boys, which can help them to read at a younger age. Despite this, all children need to grow up in their own way and at their own pace. There is no value whatsoever in pushing a girl to read before she is ready to do so. Nevertheless, all children find learning to read easier if they are familiar with books, are interested in what they can learn from them, enjoy just looking at the pictures and associate books with an intimacy with people they're close to—male and female. Grandparents, parents, aunts and uncles, step-parents, boyfriends and girlfriends are all people who may have a special relationship with a girl, can make her feel special and loved, and help her become a fluent reader by sharing books with her.

Parents

- Young girls are usually happier with stories than boys, who usually prefer factual books. Nonfiction will enhance your daughter's general knowledge and attention to detail, and fiction, her literacy and imagination.
- Reserve bedtime reading for pleasure—she'll be far too tired to learn at the end of the day.
- Girls often read less in their teens, when friends and freedom beckon. Try reading alongside her, with her music playing, to recreate the earlier cozy intimacy. If this encourages her, she may even decide to read some of her book aloud to you.

Teachers

- Choose a range of subjects for class reading that will suit boys and girls in turn, but recognize the benefits of fiction.
- Develop paired and shared reading programs that train unconfident, though competent, readers to assist younger or weaker ones.
- Use book displays and other means to portray reading as a male and female activity.
- Girls and boys alike enjoy poetry, especially humorous verse. It can be a useful introduction to more formal literature.

68 Show interest, but don't be intrusive

My father never once came to a parent–teacher meeting, to watch a game or see me in a play. He thought he'd done his part by earning the money to pay the bills. It bothered me a lot, and I ended up dropping out.

This girl had successful parents. Her mother was interested, but her father wasn't. She obviously wanted both parents to know about everything she did that was special and significant to her.

It doesn't take much to show an interest in what your daughter is doing: a question or two to initiate a conversation and follow up a point; a small moment out of the day to connect with her life and thoughts. Attending evening meetings, sporting events, and so on takes a little more effort, especially if it means leaving work early, but going out of your way and being there build a feeling in a child that she's important to you and that you take her school and her learning seriously.

But adults can reach the point where they ask too many questions, often for the wrong reasons. Children can then clam up, seeing the questions as an intrusive inquisition.

Parents

- Ask the right questions for the right reasons. Ask something directly or leave well enough alone. Don't try to get information deviously, because your daughter will figure out what you're up to, then shut you out.
- Wait for her to tell you her exam or test results. Don't make them the first thing you ask about.
- At the end of the day, instead of asking, "What happened at school today?" tell her what you did, and then say, "Do you want to tell me anything about your day?"
- Pointed questions about grades, getting into trouble, or what she did after school speak volumes about the issues on your mind.

Teachers

- When you want parents to attend special events, don't rely on student messengers: Use mail or telephone to ensure that all parents have the opportunity to attend.
- At orientations or parent–teacher evenings, and in school newsletters, constantly emphasize the important role that parents can play in their children's academic success.
- Stress that a positive role model is vital.
- Find time to take an interest in certain personal things that are important to your students, but don't persist if this makes any of them uncomfortable.

69 Develop persistence: Help her to follow through

My daughter is in college now, but she still calls me up in a panic when she's got an important essay to write, and exam time is even worse. She loses her confidence completely, and then she begins to question what life's all about.

Girls tend to be more persistent, dogged and dutiful than boys. They seem to be able to defer rewards longer, are less likely to be bored and are more tolerant of unstimulating teaching. The move toward coursework and projects as part of national testing standards suits girls well.

However, most girls have times when they doubt themselves. Their vulnerability is their self-belief rather than their stamina. Exams bring any lack of confidence to the surface.

The best-laid plans can come to nothing without persistence. Her motivation can be strong, the goal can be clear, but if your daughter doesn't have the confidence to stay on track when she feels under pressure, the work she has already invested may be wasted.

Parent

• If your daughter gets stuck, empower her. Don't belittle her or give her the answers, but help her find them herself, to give her the confidence to do it on her own next time. Then back off.

• At any sign she is losing steam, show interest and ask her to read or show you what she's done, or tell you what she has enjoyed and what's been hard.

• Check that she believes the goal is achievable, and that she has a practical plan.

• Reinforce her self-belief in every aspect of her life whenever you can.

Teachers

• All children find it easier to concentrate if work and rewards are delivered in short, quick chunks. Give goals a high profile and make the paths to each one clear, so that interest does not wane.

• If a student gets stuck or loses interest, jointly prepare a clear plan to get her back on track.

• Make sure a girl knows why a piece of work is good, so she can't write it off as a fluke and maintain her low opinion of herself.

• Don't constantly move the goal-posts farther away. To gain real confidence, girls need to feel that they are on top of their work, not constantly struggling to attain a higher goal.

70 Support the school

Although for the most part girls today do well academically, they are growing up exposed to a culture that questions the value of academic success and to an economic climate that offers instant fortunes and makes exams seem irrelevant. The temptation not to play the school's game is great, and not every girl will succeed academically. We can't change that culture, but we can model the importance of learning as a lifelong process and accept that home and school need to support each other, in partnership.

If parents respect schools, and schools respect parents, there will be fewer cracks for girls to fall through, particularly during the earth-moving time of adolescence. Parents who distance themselves from their daughters' school not only create split loyalties, but also make it easier for girls to team up with the troublemakers rather than the teachers.

Parents

- Talk up your daughter's school, not down. Avoid complaining about it in front of her, even if you're paying fees that are too high or having a political debate.
- Whenever possible, both parents should attend meetings about their daughter's progress in school. An absent parent can call the teacher for a summary.
- Try to be free to watch your daughter take part in school events. Avoid saying, "Not another thing that school/club wants me to do!" or she wants you to do.
- Attending fund-raising events with her will help her to feel part of the school.
- Help her to remember and gather the things she's been asked to bring to school.

Teachers

- Try to let parents know when things are going well, not only when there are problems. When parents feel proud of their daughters, they usually treat them better.
- Take parents' worries seriously, and respond to their concerns with respect.
- Avoid appearing to criticize a girl's parents: "Didn't your mom check that you had everything?"
- Focus parents' evenings on what parents can actively do to help their girls set appropriate goals. Stress the importance of relaxation, too.

71 Respect her teachers

It's much harder now than when I started teaching twenty-five years ago. It's not so much the constant changes in what we're expected to teach or the extra paperwork; it is the parents and the students, who show us so little respect now. When children hear parents putting us down at home, it's hard for them to accept our authority and take work seriously when they're here.

Children will not make the effort to listen and concentrate if they do not trust or respect their teacher. Constant complaining about teachers, especially about a particular one, will encourage disrespect and challenging behavior at school.

Schools and parents need to work together as partners, respecting each other, not fighting or criticizing one another.

Parents

- At all times, try to put across the teacher's perspective and be realistic about his or her commitments, even if you side with your daughter.
- Teachers are people, too. They have personal lives and sometimes go through hard times. They like to hear good news as well as bad. Most do their best.
- Don't be timid about telling a teacher what seems to work best for your daughter. They can't know everything.
- It's only fair to the teacher and your daughter to tell the school if there's a problem at home that might affect her behavior or work in school.

Teachers

- We should all have to earn the respect we feel is our due. Try to see things from the parents' angle. Don't put them down.
- Be aware that vulnerable parents are likely to take your treatment of their daughter personally, as if it's directed at them. Respecting every girl in your care contributes to respectful home–school relationships.
- Send home good news, not just bad.
- During parent–teacher conferences, take parents' concerns seriously and end with, "Is there anything else?" Arrange an alternative time for discussion if the issue demands it.

72 Channel competition creatively

Most girls have a competitive urge. Channeled reasonably, sensitively and creatively, it can be used to develop motivation, achievement and a positive sense of self. Exploited carelessly, it may lead to anxiety, despair, doubt and a decision to give up on trying to do well.

Girls do best when they are encouraged to compete against themselves, when they focus on improving their last best performance, because this keeps their self-esteem intact. Competition is potentially dangerous when girls perform to impress their friends or adults, set their sights on beating others and invest their self-worth in the result. Even though a girl may have tried really hard and prepared well, others may have tried harder or simply have more natural talent. Whenever the result is not completely within her personal control, there is the chance that anxiety will threaten a girl's self-confidence and increase the likelihood of a poor performance.

Parents

- It is better to identify a specific goal ("Try to improve the grade on your science quizzes") than a general one ("Go for the honor roll this time").
- Don't fuel competition between brothers and sisters. Each child needs to be successful in her own way, and to be accepted unconditionally for who she is.
- Avoid competing against your daughter, especially if you intend it as a spur to greater effort.
- Fun competitions are fine: "See if you can beat me to the top of the stairs" is a great way to get children on the road to bed.

Teachers

- Research shows that classrooms run competitively produce anxious children.
- Encourage students to perform in order to improve, not to impress. Give them feedback, too, so that they can see the progress they have made.
- Cooperative games enable children to have fun without winning or losing. Try playing musical chairs in two ways: first, as usual, removing chairs and children each round; then removing only chairs, which means that children have to sit on top of each other. Ask which version they prefer.

73 Failure lights the path to success

All girls experience failure—lots of it. A girl will almost certainly fail at her first attempt at walking; she won't master buttons on her first fumble, ride a bike or tie her shoes right away, yet she is prepared to give it another try. Why don't these early failures make growing girls give up, despite sometimes intense frustration, while later ones can stop them in their tracks and throw them into the depths of misery?

The uncomfortable truth is that adults are often responsible for the change. They scold children for failing, tease them and make them feel ashamed.

Yet failure is not something to be shunned. It provides neutral information about what went wrong and what needs to be put right. Failure is an inevitable and essential part of learning, and it shows that learning is happening at the frontier of current knowledge. If the lessons that underlie failure are taken to heart, the errors light the path to success. But it won't happen if adults deny, ignore or punish failures, making a girl feel she needs to cheat, hide the truth or run from it herself.

Parents

- Respond constructively— failure is like a puzzle to be solved, not a disaster to be denied. Consider whether the goal was too ambitious.
- Respond sincerely. Be honest and ensure that it remains your daughter's problem, not yours.
- Respond sensitively. However much she may deny it, failure is upsetting and can undermine confidence. Accept, understand and let her voice her feelings. Don't be too strict with her for a while. Help her to feel successful in other ways.
- Show that you love her for who she is, not for what she can do.
- Don't punish her for failing— she may start to lie or cheat.

Teachers

- Describe in detail what went wrong and how she may do better.
- Let the student know that you believe she can improve. Show her how with a sample piece of work.
- Encourage her to self-evaluate as much and as accurately as possible.
- Be available if she needs help.
- Look for modest, not exceptional, success stories in which individual girls can explain how, and perhaps why, they overcame failure.
- Try to discover the reasons behind any unexpected fall in performance.

74 Watch her doing something she enjoys

When I got older, my mom didn't go ice skating with me anymore because I went with my friends. I kept getting better, then one day I made her come again because I really wanted her to see how good I was. I'd started from nothing and I was so proud.

Anything that is important to us, we want to share. Children are the same. Children usually enjoy doing the things they do well, so one reason to watch your daughter is to let her show off a little and accept the pride she feels in her achievement. Watching brings you further into her life. The simple fact that you are there increases togetherness and helps her to feel comfortable with herself.

Whether your daughter enjoys rollerblading, ice skating, conquering playground equipment, dressing up, acting, computing or playing a musical instrument, watch her. It may take some effort, but she will thrive in the warmth your sharing will bring.

Parents

- Find the time to watch your daughter.
- "Mom, can I show you how I . . . ?" or "Dad, come and see me do . . ." should be answered with "Sure" (preferably not with "later" added).
- Let your daughter impress you. Tell her afterward how much you enjoyed watching her.
- Tell somebody else, such as a grandparent, how well she's doing, when she can overhear, so that she can feel proud of her skills. If no one's available, you can say, "Your Grandma would have loved to see you do that."

Teachers

- You can't watch what the girls in your class do in their personal time, but you can find a moment to ask them to tell you about something they have done.
- Try to value whatever it is students enjoy doing or achieving.
- Provided that family and work commitments allow, it can be gratifying for students to see teachers attending musical or sporting events.

75 Don't invest your self-worth in her success

Every time I did well at something, my mom would rush off and tell the whole neighborhood. She treated it as her achievement, and I ended up feeling used, empty and angry.

When a parent's self-esteem depends on, or is disproportionately enhanced by, a daughter's success, this imposes upon her a heavy responsibility that no child should have to bear. Although parents and teachers naturally feel good when their daughters and students do well, it is dangerous when adults begin to rely on a child's achievements for their own sense of self-worth.

Such behavior can damage a girl's self-esteem in a number of subtle ways. If parents feel good about themselves only when their child succeeds, they are, in effect, stealing success from that child. This will leave her feeling used, confused and empty instead of fulfilled. Only further, and repeated, success will replenish her sense of achievement, which leads to the burden of perfectionism. She will also come to believe that she is valued solely for what she can do, not for who she is.

Parents

- If you want to tell other people about your daughter's achievements, think about whom you want to tell, consider why and ask for her permission to do so first.
- Avoid setting a new goal for your daughter as soon as she has reached one. (Maybe you benefit in some way from this pressure you put on her?)
- Consider whether you have different expectations for your sons and your daughters, and whether you identify more closely with one or the other for some reason.
- Tell yourself firmly that it's *her* success, the result of *her* effort and hers to hold on to and share if she chooses.

Teachers

- Good teachers deliver more than results. To keep yourself from focusing too narrowly on them, at a time when there's every incentive to do so, list other ways in which you want your students to develop and achieve.
- If you think you may have become success dependent, reflect on the other things you are good at and that give you pleasure.
- If one group's results are not good, and you find yourself getting depressed as a result, put yourself back in control. Consider what you could do differently next time that might change the outcome.

76 Let her be responsible for her own success—and failure

The moment of victory is far too short to live for that alone.
—Martina Navratilova, tennis champion

Success and failure tend to be overlaid with moral significance—it is good to succeed and shameful to fail. Parents can be affected, too, so that if their daughter succeeds, it is their success, and if she fails, it is their failure. This tendency to take ownership is damaging as well as confusing.

When parents take responsibility for a girl's success, they effectively steal it from her, which may lead her to fail in the future. A mother might appropriate her daughter's success to make herself feel good, and run to tell others; or she might take credit for it, implying that it would not have happened without her input. If her success is always taken from her, a girl may eventually turn on her tormentors and refuse to play, or she may burn out.

Taking responsibility for a daughter's failure is equally unhelpful. Your shame may lead to punishment or trivialization. Either will prevent a daughter from learning from mistakes and progressing.

Parents

- Have realistic expectations of your daughter and accept her unconditionally.
- See success as neutral feedback: You can acknowledge it, but glory shouldn't come into it.
- Help your daughter to feel comfortable with her feelings of delight or disappointment, frustration or sadness.
- If her failures become your personal shame, you hinder her chances of recovery.
- Mistakes are a sign that she's at the frontiers of her knowledge. Discuss why they happened and what she can do differently next time.
- Your daughter's success is hers, not yours. Don't take the credit.

Teachers

- Always congratulate a student on her success and hand her the credit.
- Explain in detail what she has done right, so that she knows how to repeat it next time.
- Offer her some unpressured time at her new level, time to adjust to and accept her success; then wait to see whether she progresses on her own initiative.
- Take the shame out of failure. Personal ridicule will encourage students to hide behind excuses.

CHAPTER 8

Encouraging Confidence and Independence

We are moving from a "to be or not to be" generation to a "to have or not to have" generation.

—Trond Waage, Norway's Ombudsman for Children

True happiness, it has been said, is not a destination, but a way of traveling. Whether you have it depends on how comfortable you are with yourself. This is the inner confidence that is called *self-esteem.* "Happiness is self-contentedness," wrote the Greek philosopher Aristotle.

The consumer society may give children injections of pleasure, but it tends to reduce the opportunities they have to discover who they really are. The more a young girl follows fashion or a group, the less certain she is about her own preferences or inclinations. The less she looks over her shoulder to check her acceptability to others, the more confident and independent she will be.

Confidence, of course, ebbs and flows. We can feel confident in some situations and terrified in others, relaxed with some people and uncertain with others. Confidence also dips naturally at certain times as part of normal child development. Girls' self-esteem plummets at fourteen, the age at which boys express themselves most freely, and boys reach their lowest level at nineteen. In recent studies of girls' and boys' confidence and self-esteem, researchers found that while, overall, fewer girls express confidence than boys (21 percent to boys' 25), more girls than boys were in the middle or the very confident ranges, and fewer girls than boys had low self-confidence (12 percent to boys' 8).

A girl with confidence will know her own mind, honor and care for her body, be aware of her capabilities, have trust and faith and the ability to give pleasure to others. If she can make sense of her immediate world, she will be able to go out into the wider one with hope, purpose, passion and direction.

Confidence does not come from believing you are perfect, but from knowing you are good enough and have more to give. If you like enough of yourself, you are able to live with the parts that are less endearing. When you know you are good at some things, you can acknowledge, with no loss to your self-image, that you are not so good at others, and you can face the world with honesty and humility.

Your daughter will grow in confidence and independence if you first show confidence and trust in her, offer her security and certainty, and give her time and attention so that she can believe in herself.

77 Offer her safety, security and predictability

The Concise Oxford Dictionary defines "confidence" as "firm trust; assured expectation; self-reliance; boldness."

Nobody can develop self-confidence if they neither trust themselves nor have the assured expectation that other people's behavior is trustworthy and predictable. Girls who do not have a measure of consistency and predictability in their lives will find it hard to acquire the necessary trust, in others or in themselves, to become either truly self-confident or genuinely independent. When adults behave in an arbitrary and neglectful way, they undermine a child's confidence and generate emotional dependency.

Routines help to create both trust and security. If a girl's key caregivers clearly trust her and provide consistency, she can begin to trust herself, her judgment, and the behavior of other people. Parents don't make a daughter independent by disappearing from her life and letting her fend for herself, but by being there for her.

Parents

• Try to ensure that your daughter begins each day with a clear idea of what will happen and when, either in terms of routines and events or whom she will meet.

• As much as possible, arrange for her to see any nonresident parent regularly and reliably.

• Make your own behavior toward her as reliable and predictable as you can. If you have mood changes, or your routine has to change, try to explain why.

• Consider whether you could change your own or her commitments to increase the sense of pattern and "assured expectation" in her life.

Teachers

• All children feel safer when lessons have a clear structure and purpose, when goals and objectives are clear at the start.

• Clearly structured tasks will encourage students to speak and listen in a purposeful way and will help them gain confidence in thinking constructively and creatively.

• Let students know well in advance if there will be any changes to the normal school routine or lesson plan.

78 Nurture her social skills

Girls, typically, not only talk more than boys as they play, but seem more ready to make and trust friends. Their brains also give them a natural verbal advantage. All these things encourage good social and communication skills.

These skills help to give girls a secure and happy future, socially and economically. Employers are increasingly looking for people who are polite and respectful; can work together in teams; can reflect on, discuss and sell their ideas; and can handle disagreements with skill. Young people who grow up able to share, compromise and be flexible, and who have an understanding of how others think and feel, will have a head start. They are also more likely to have happier and longer-term personal relationships, which so often flop when differences are not managed either constructively or safely.

The best way to help your daughter become socially confident is to ensure there is plenty of fun, conversation, discussion and respectful listening within the family.

Parents

- Involve your daughter in your social life whenever appropriate. It will show that you enjoy her company and trust her to behave well.
- Try to be sociable yourself. If she sees you mixing confidently with others, she'll learn from you.
- Encourage friendships. Invite friends over and see if there's a social or sports group she can join. Ration solitary activities, such as computer games.
- Reading will develop her reflective powers and insight. Talk to her as much as you can: Ask for her views, tell her what you've been doing—and actively listen to her when she talks to you.

Teachers

- Include paired and small-group work in your lessons so that students learn to listen to, talk to, respect and compromise with others.
- In mixed classes, make sure that girls work with boys, so that they pick up alternative ways of thinking, doing and learning.
- Seating arrangements are important. Whom they sit next to can matter a lot to students.
- Encourage discussion, listening and reflection. When children get into the habit of thinking before they write, their work standard rises significantly.

79 Offer chances to test herself

Confidence flows from competence. When a girl possesses a variety of skills that she can rely on in different situations, she will feel confident and capable. She will expect success instead of anticipating failure when faced with obstacles.

The more skills she acquires, the more competent she will feel; but she won't become competent at anything if she watches a lot of television or is told endlessly that she's no good when she does try something. Beware of gender stereotyping when you recommend activities for your daughter to try. She should spend plenty of time outdoors, playing and running around, to develop her strength, coordination and long-term health.

At the right time, a taste of the world of work may help her to become confident about her goals. Schools increasingly organize this, but further experience can only be beneficial, especially if she can join you and appreciate the responsibilities you have outside the home.

Parents

- Every journey begins with a first step. Your daughter won't be as good as you, but she'll need to feel competent from the beginning. Teasing her for failing will undermine her confidence.
- Vacation activities, such as camp, and afterschool clubs can introduce girls to a range of new skills.
- Involve your daughter in the jobs you do—cooking, cleaning, car washing, weeding, do-it-yourself projects, paying the bills—and be patient if they take longer to do.
- Let her try out her thoughts and judgments on you. Invite them, hear them and respect them. Don't dominate or compete.

Teachers

- Girls relish responsibility and like to seize the opportunity to take it. Make sure that the boys in your class are not left out.
- Encourage a girl who seems to lack friends, confidence and social skills to attend any afterschool clubs available.

80 Work to and from her strengths

Any girl will learn more easily, perform better and be more self-motivated if she can do things in a way that suits her and interests her. Some children learn better by looking at visual images, some when sounds are used and some through touch. A child's all-important sense of mastery—how effective and competent she feels—will develop best when she is allowed to start from who, and where, she is.

Success breeds success. All educators know that when a child succeeds in one field, she will have a more positive attitude toward the next challenge she has to face.

When you can acknowledge your daughter's strengths, she will feel not only understood but also accepted, which will free her to learn and develop in her own way. The more you impose your own methods and ignore hers, the more likely she is to lose the confidence and ability to work independently.

Parents

• Identify your daughter's skills and strengths. Concentrate on what she can do, not on what she can't.

• Don't belittle the talent that is special to her.

• Think about her preferred approach to working and learning, and her particular passions. Don't force her to work in ways that are hard for her.

Teachers

• Discover her passion, apply it to your subject and let her fly. All children concentrate better when they're confident, committed and interested.

• Quizzes can make learning fun and help girls become more comfortable with risk-taking and uncertainty.

• Young girls' play is often less vigorous, and more verbal and fluent, than boys', but there are always quiet boys and boisterous girls who cross the boundaries. Don't label girls who prefer rough or athletic play as "tomboys."

81 Give her independence, but don't abandon her

Independence and responsibility should be given to children when they are ready and not be granted only because it is convenient for an adult to do so. Take into consideration the child's age, maturity and wishes. Sometimes, a family's practical needs are the trigger for granting further independence, and it comes at the right time. However, it is important to judge whether giving your daughter extra freedom or responsibility is simply a convenience for you, and to be aware of your daughter's possible view of your motives. She should not be given too much too soon, be exploited or be left feeling abandoned. She may appear able to cope, but in reality she may still feel she needs your company, guidance and attention, but be too proud to say so. And if she becomes anxious or feels out of her depth, her confidence will be weakened, not strengthened.

Parents

- The first few times your daughter does something new, stay close by or within easy reach so she knows she's not entirely on her own.
- Apply the idea of "supported independence" to assess whether she might feel abandoned or neglected. Check whether her friends are available and reliable for times when you cannot be contacted to provide support if needed.
- Ask for her honest opinion about the arrangements you made for the resolution of potential problems or in preparation for her traveling, being or coping on her own.

Teachers

- Independent learning is a valuable approach, but students will continue to need support.
- Girls may need help with time management. For projects with a long deadline, arrange to be available for consultation at scheduled times well before the due date.
- Offer "bite-size" chunks: Suggest interim deadlines for sections of work to prevent any student from falling behind.
- Do not assign tasks and responsibilities without clear guidelines.
- When students work on their own, encourage them to think ahead about areas where they might need help.

82 Monitor and supervise, from a distance

One night I was due home by eleven. My friends and I cooked up other plans, so I called home with some made-up story about why I needed to stay the night with one of them. Mom just did not buy it and stuck to her guns. Afterward, I was glad. I realized I wasn't sure what might have happened that night.

Research shows that many girls who get into trouble with the police are out for long periods of time without having to report their comings and goings to anyone at home. Monitoring and supervision help keep girls on track when they are exploring their newfound freedom, but parents should watch over their daughters sensitively and from a distance, so that the girls don't feel insulted by any perceived lack of trust.

Keeping yourself informed of your daughter's movements is vital. It helps to keep her safe, because she knows that you're aware and that you care. If you cast her adrift, she may flounder, feel neglected, and then get back at you by seeking trouble.

Parents

- Discuss with your daughter times for calling and coming home every time she goes out. Afterward, casually ask what happened and how things went.
- If you are worried, check with one of her friends' parents that they were told the same story—make sure you have these contact numbers.
- If she's late, find out why, so that she knows you notice and care. If possible, wait up for her and see how she is.
- Take a look at the club or place where she goes, to get a sense of its atmosphere.
- Keep an eye on her bedroom in case it gives clues about any work or personal problems, although do not cross the line of personal privacy.

Teachers

- Be alert to any pattern in missed deadlines. Consult with colleagues if you are worried.
- Patrolling children closely won't help them learn to manage and monitor themselves. Keep an eye open at break times, but from an appropriate distance.
- It is easy to keep records of students' grades for class and homework, of late arrivals and of major incidents, but it's important to keep track of other less obvious things that may indicate personal trouble, such as tears, visits to the school nurse and changes in personal appearance.

83 Encourage responsibility and safe risk-taking

Research shows that from birth onward, girls are more calm than boys, more thoughtful and cautious and less inclined to take risks. They are also more likely to please. These tendencies may make them easier to handle when they are younger. However, as they approach adolescence, their stronger attachment to their family can make it more difficult for them to achieve independence. This may explain why girls seem more prone to the "tempestuous teens" than boys.

When girls are given freedom all at once, or when they have torn themselves free in anger from families that have restricted them, their risk-taking can be dangerous. Of course, our daughters may get into trouble even if we have, we believe, prepared them well—the more freedom they have, the bigger their potential mistakes. Nevertheless, the best preparation for safe risk-taking we can provide is to let them know we care, to treat them fairly, to encourage their thinking skills and self-respect and, most crucial, to see that their responsibilities grow in proportion to their rights.

Parents

- When your daughter asks for more independence, try to give it to her. If you feel the particular freedom she seeks is not appropriate, discuss an alternative change that will satisfy her. She'll then have less need to struggle free and prove herself in irresponsible ways.
- Be tolerant of her mistakes. Harsh punishments may make her behave more irresponsibly.
- Rights matched by responsibilities can encourage safer behavior, but all girls will take risks at some point. Discuss what you mean by safe risk-taking, and ensure that her freedom is set within clear limits.

Teachers

- Learning involves taking responsibility and taking risks. When kept in balance, this offers useful lessons for life.
- Challenging girls, or those with low self-esteem, may respond well to being given special tasks and more responsibilities.
- Girls who undertake death-defying acts of bravado can be mirroring the lack of care they perceive in close adults. Be attuned to the reasons behind high-risk behavior.
- Address safe limits to risk-taking in social studies classes and school assemblies. Discuss the attraction of thrill and excitement and what these achieve.

84 Encourage self-management

When parents of our new kindergarteners first come into school, we explain why we like them to encourage self-care skills in their children. It's partly because we have so many coats to button up, but mainly because it has vital educational value. Young children who can take care of themselves are more confident, responsible, independent and effective in their work.

It can be hard to let go. With such busy lives, we may feel we don't have enough opportunities to demonstrate our love and commitment. One remaining way, as daughters grow older and get harder to hug, is to tend to their needs. I met one glamorous mother in her fifties who was still buying clothes for her two daughters, even though they were both away at college, because she felt uncomfortable about their lack of style. She was even happy to return the items if they were rejected. But it is not helpful to do everything for a child. It fosters dependency and will prevent a girl from learning to organize her work, time, money and image for herself.

Parents

- Encourage financial independence: Give your daughter a regular allowance or a clothes allowance, and stick to it.
- Encourage organizational skills: For example, if you're planning to go out together, as a fun project, ask her to find out the opening times and costs. Give her a budget and charge of the money.
- Even young girls can be encouraged to put on their shoes, wash their faces, brush their teeth and get their things ready for school by themselves.
- Don't back off altogether. Do enough to let her know that you still care and think about her.

Teachers

- Make sure parents are aware that children who can take care of themselves are also more successful learners.
- Don't be tempted to let a few competent students do all the responsible jobs. Spread the tasks among all students.
- Girls who live between two sets of parents may have trouble remembering books, especially early in the separation. It's better to give a child two sets than to scold her and add to her problems.
- Be rigorous in promoting the use of calendars and homework planners.
- Actively address time and stress management and work and planning skills.

85 Let her say no

Self-esteem gives girls the power to say no—to their friends or to an adult who is behaving in a frightening or strange way. Girls who are expected to be "good" all the time and who rely on other people's approval to feel accepted will find it much harder to withdraw from potential danger when this could result in being teased, scolded or cold-shouldered.

Sound self-confidence is one path to staying safe, and parents and other caregivers will therefore need to nurture self-esteem as the core of confidence. But girls will also need a little practice. They can't turn from habitual "yes" girls into fierce "no" girls in one step. Many parents may feel, not without reason, that their daughters are already too sassy and willful and need no further encouragement. But insolence and opposition are not exactly what is required. Children do need to be allowed to disagree; to learn to stand up for themselves with sound argument, not fists; and to know that their judgment is worthy of respect.

Parents

- Let your daughter have views that differ from your own, so that she feels confident about being in a minority of one when necessary.
- Allow her to express her feelings. If it's OK to feel angry, sad or excited at home, it will be easier for her to respond honestly and decisively in potentially dangerous situations.
- Let her know you trust her judgment.
- Listen to her properly when she wants to tell you something.
- Respect her choice of friends whenever possible. If you criticize too often, she's more likely to ignore you when you have serious concerns.

Teachers

- Employers no longer need armies of robots or lines of lemmings. Ritual obedience is out of date, though politeness and respect certainly are not. Older children, especially, must be given the space to make up their own minds.
- Listen. You don't have to give in to show respect to a student's right to see things differently and to say so, provided that she expresses herself politely.
- Explore the scope for compromise. She may have a good case, which you can answer in another way.

86 Teach coping and survival skills

The best way to learn to handle many problems is through experience. Experience lessens fear and also helps to build common sense. Hiding from fears makes them grow. Staying at home or in a car does not build life or street skills, and protecting girls from the world is not responsible parenting. Getting out and about with your daughter, walking, cycling and taking public transportion teach geographical sense and street awareness. Going out for night walks will help her to respect, but not fear, the dark.

Staying indoors does not encourage physical fitness. The two best defenses against bullying and other dangers are strong bodies and inner confidence. When girls are fit, physically strong and have good posture, it helps them not only to run away or wriggle free but also to look confident and convey to others they are someone who is best left alone.

Discuss different coping strategies with your daughter, particularly ways to reduce risk and protect herself in potentially dangerous situations.

Parents

- Useful risk-reduction advice includes staying in public view and in populated places; avoiding back stairs and alleys; going out in a group—preferably composed of people you know and trust—and not getting separated from them; carrying money safely, with a small amount in a purse or wallet and the rest elsewhere.

- Practice verbal responses: A sharp word delivered quickly is probably safer than a punch.

- Before she goes out, ask your daughter if she's worried about anything. If she is, discuss it.

- It's important that she feels confident. Don't undermine her by predicting disaster.

Teachers

- If it is practical, organize a "walk-to-school" day or week.

- Include safety and survival issues in physical education lessons, but keep all discussions as positive as possible: Fear of "stranger danger" can get out of hand and destroy children's confidence.

87 Enter the forbidden zone

Sex, alcohol and—increasingly—drugs in every form are an inevitable part of growing up for girls today. Do not allow these topics to become censored areas in your family. Although your daughter needs her private space as she enters her teens and will defend this sometimes aggressively against your intrusion, and even though it's hard to strike the right note and avoid embarrassment, it is important to keep talking. Communication must be maintained, so that if serious problems arise regarding sexual behavior or alcohol or drug abuse, you can address these straightforwardly, because the territory is familiar.

By the age of fourteen, research tells us, one in three young people will have tried at least one form of recreational drug. If you don't talk to your daughter about drugs, someone else will. Telling a girl not to do something when peer pressure is strong may not have much impact, but suggesting that she stay in control of, and true to, herself by doing things only when it feels right for her may give her that ounce of extra courage to say no.

Parents

- At home, try to talk openly and comfortably about sex in general conversation, so that the subject is not unfamiliar or taboo.
- If it has become difficult to talk to your daughter, leaflets and books about safe sex, drinking and drug use are available from schools, clinics and community and national programs.
- Be quietly vigilant. Become informed about and watch out for signs of inappropriate behavior or use of either drugs or alcohol.
- If you begin a new relationship during your daughter's puberty, be aware that she may find the sexual side of it problematic. Be discreet, don't compete.

Teachers

- Most schools, from grade school to high school, have sex and drug education programs. These need to be given high status and presented by a qualified staff member or outside expert: Someone with the right interpersonal and professional skills and knowledge.
- Teaching should reinforce high self-esteem and good social and communication skills as the best defenses against premature sexual activity, early pregnancy, and drug use.
- Teachers who lead sex and drug discussions should possess excellent group-work skills to enable all students to participate comfortably and confidently and take the subject seriously.

88 Promote self-direction

People don't resist change, they resist being changed.

—Gerard Nierenberg

One form of independence is self-direction. Children who are self-directed know what they want to achieve and can knuckle down and manage tasks and problems independently without relying on adult supervision. This helps them to experience autonomy, because they have enough control over aspects of their lives to feel powerful (not passive). They also experience a sense of authenticity so that they are able to make their actions follow their thoughts. Girls who are given no chance to direct themselves, or who lack the skills or confidence to do so, feel helpless. And when they feel helpless, they soon feel hopeless.

Self-direction and independence reinforce each other. The more self-directed girls are, the better they can manage independence. The more independence they are given, the more likely they are to become confident and self-reliant, to show initiative and to be creative. However, make it clear to your daughter that although you are promoting self-reliance, she can still come to you if things go wrong and she needs advice.

Parents

• Directive parents create dependency: The more you tell your daughter what to do, the less competent she will feel and the more she will need you to continue directing her.

• Give her an allowance as soon as she can handle it. Then she can make financial decisions without reference to you.

• When children feel helpless, they soon feel hopeless.

• If you feel that your daughter should change in some way, involve her in deciding when and how. If she wants to change something, cooperate.

• To become self-directed, girls need time that's theirs alone. Filling your daughter's every moment denies her this learning opportunity.

Teachers

• Students improve when they understand how to make progress: Set clear objectives and goals.

• A student will feel more in control of what she has to do if you ask, "Do you want to do it this way, or that way?"

• Once she has a goal, ask how she plans to reach it.

• Encourage her to think, plan ahead and manage her own time, meeting her needs and yours.

• Encourage self-appraisal as part of the process.

CHAPTER 9

Checking Out Your Role and Feelings

This is where we come back to basics. Despite a growing emphasis on both the power of genes and the acknowledged pull of the peer group, parents and other key caring adults are in a strong position to influence a girl and to affect how much faith she has in herself, how competent she feels and thus the overall quality of her self-esteem. A child can be born with a predisposition to be positive about life and herself, or with a negative tendency. Close adults can either build her up or undermine her. A family may have two daughters who couldn't be more different from each other, but one may need a lot more support than the other. It is our role as adults to provide, as much as possible, the conditions within which each one can feel secure and capable, not uncertain and incapable. She must be able to influence her life, not merely react to events and be a victim. She needs values, a direction and the capacity to enjoy activities, causes and people, not to be rootless, isolated or completely self-absorbed.

We can influence but we cannot control all outcomes or even always handle our own behavior as we would like. Outside factors intervene. Stress, uncertainty and change prevent us from giving as much as the job of parenting requires sometimes. Frequently, our daughter's behavior will test us to our limits. She contributes to the relationship dynamic, too, and, as she approaches adulthood, she must be held increasingly accountable for her own behavior. If, however, we have provided most of the basics, accepted her imperfections as well as our own, demonstrated our commitment in a way that satisfied her, and bolstered her confidence whenever she became vulnerable, we have given her a firm foundation that will help her to cope confidently with any future setback.

Our feelings, hopes, and fears inevitably color what we say and do. No human being is sufficiently saintly to think about someone else's interests all the time, to the exclusion of their own. Children demand, and need, a great deal of time and attention. Giving as much as they sometimes want takes a lot out of parents. Indeed, children can take so much out that you may wonder whether you have anything left. If you do not consciously take the time regularly to replenish yourself, recharge your batteries and develop your own sense of self-confidence, you may find you build protective barriers around yourself in a desperate and arbitrary way. The barriers may help you to hold on to yourself, but you may also cut yourself off from your daughter when she needs you most.

The best way to help children grow up happy and healthy is to make sure that you also continue growing and enjoy your life within and outside of your family.

89 Cherish and trust yourself

At the same time as you take care of your daughter, you have to take care of yourself. You probably don't need to be told that the better you feel about yourself, the better you cope with challenge and problems and the nicer you are to those around you. You will know, too, that when you have had a bad day or are very tired, you are more likely to take it out on your nearest and dearest. Taking care of yourself is an investment that benefits others, because when you behave well and notice good things that others are doing, you help them to feel as good as you do. Good behavior is infectious.

It can be hard to trust your competence during every stage that children pass through and to handle every issue that arises. Most parents and teachers have a favorite age for children that they enjoy more than others. While teachers can choose whether to teach little ones or older children, parents have no choice: They have to cope throughout. You may often doubt yourself, but remember that children value firmness. Discuss any uncertainty with others, carefully review your first reactions and if you still feel the same, trust your own judgment.

Parents

• Talk to others. It usually helps. Try joining a local parenting group.

• Identify your little luxury, the thing that calms you down and restores your faith in yourself: It may be reading a trashy book, going to the movies or having a drink with friends.

• Make sure your choice of a pick-me-up is realistic. When grandiose schemes fail, it can be anything but rejuvenating.

• Try to treat yourself on a regular basis. Some little indulgences may fit your schedule easily, but others take longer and require planning.

• "I've always wanted to . . ."—so do it!

Teachers

• Trust and believe in yourself. If you doubt your skills, you may interpret students' problem behavior as a personal attack and react defensively, provocatively and unconstructively.

• List what you see as your professional strengths, then identify where there's room for improvement. Discuss with colleagues how to share your collective skills to aid professional development.

• Managing girls who challenge you is tiring. Rather than suffering in silence and pretending you're coping, set up a support group with colleagues to pool ideas.

• After a bad patch, pamper, don't punish, yourself.

90 Let her be different

I can't believe how different I am from my mom. She was a piano teacher, a little brainy and loved endless walks. I hated classical music, didn't like reading or school and those walks were just awful. My brother and I were dragged along, but as soon as we could, we were allowed to stay behind. She also let me give up the piano after two years. It was such a relief.

We spend the early years of our child's life treating her as a mirror—looking for ourselves in her. It starts with her face: "She's got my eyes and her dad's nose." Then you move on to her likes and dislikes: "She loves organizing her closet, just like I did." All the similarities are proof that our daughter is part of and belongs to us, so it can come as a shock later on when we are forced to accept that she is not only different, but also will go out of her way to prove it.

If you use your child to make yourself feel acceptable, she will feel shackled and stifled. Growing up is hard enough, but it will be much harder if you make your daughter responsible for your happiness.

Parents

• Give your daughter the space to be herself. It's your problem, not hers, if you feel uncomfortable about her being different.

• Don't compete with, criticize or ridicule her. Every challenge drags her into your territory and reinforces her view that you think your ways, talents and preferences are better than hers.

• Getting involved in her school is great, but don't overdo it. All girls need some space to be themselves, free from a parent's watchful and expectant eye.

• Take an interest in the music, magazines, games or clothes your daughter likes, even if each is only a passing fad. You're not expected to agree—her taste is her choice.

Teachers

• Encourage children to be aware of their individual likes and dislikes, temperament and idiosyncrasies.

• Explore class activities that highlight and develop respect and tolerance for differences.

• Vary your teaching methods. The way you feel most comfortable getting information across may not suit the learning styles of all the girls in your class, and they may be too polite or intimidated to tell you.

91 Examine your expectations

Every family has its own story and preferred way of organizing itself. These influence what we expect for ourselves and those we live with, including our children, whether or not we want them to. There is often a hidden, sometimes complicated, agenda, which children eventually detect and react to.

While we accept that education and careers are important for girls, in many families women still play a more traditional role. Some mothers will want their daughters to grasp the opportunities they never had, and some will prefer them to follow in their own footsteps. Where parents' expectations differ from each other, a girl may become further confused about the path she should take in life, especially if she usually pleases them, not herself. There is some evidence that confusion about identity may contribute to problems such as eating disorders.

Some typical stories behind parental expectations: You threw away the opportunities you had and you don't want your daughter to do the same; you are successful and see her success as another feather in your cap; you want your daughter to do what you always wanted to do, but couldn't.

Parents

- List your expectations for your daughter. Be honest about why you hold these dear and think of the possible positive and negative consequences for her for each.
- Think separately about your daughter's athletic activities, music, art, school, career, hobbies and leisure, and whether your expectations are high, medium or low for each one. If there are lots of "highs," consider where you might lower your sights.
- Ask your daughter whether she agrees with your goals and whether she feels she can, or knows how to, meet them.
- Looking at just your short-term academic expectations, consider whether they are realistic and how you will feel if she doesn't meet them.

Teachers

- Girls benefit when teachers set high, but achievable, short-term goals. Be careful that your personal goals and school goals don't put undue pressure on your students.
- Help each student define her own expectations, and step in only if she has made a serious misjudgment.

92 What you expect is what you get

"Time for school in ten minutes. Remember what you need and I'll see you at the front door at quarter to." For older girls, this is a far more helpful and positive approach than "You only have ten minutes. Have you got your homework? Have you brushed your teeth? Don't forget your lunch, and don't be late like you were yesterday!"

Girls who feel trusted by an adult feel proud of that trust and work at keeping it. They live up to expectations to strengthen it further. Research shows consistently that high expectations of behavior produce good results, and low expectations produce poor ones. "What you see is what you get" is shorthand for this process. "What you see" in this case is your perception of your daughter's personality and behavior. "What you get" is the behavior you expect based on this perception. So if you ask a girl to do something in a way that assumes and expects that she will comply, you are more likely to get the result you want. The reverse is also true: When you let slip that you think your daughter will not cooperate or succeed at something, she probably won't.

Parents

- Stay positive: Notice, constantly, what your daughter does right. If she fails to do something, restate the request or expectation. Don't berate her.
- Stop predicting or assuming poor performance or behavior with phrases such as, "I expect you'll fail this test, too," or even "You will be good, won't you?"
- Avoid sticking labels on her, especially negative ones, such as "naughty," "cheat," "liar," "hopeless;" give her hope and faith in herself.
- Beware of asking too much of her and therefore becoming her central reference point, which should be herself.

Teachers

- Have appropriate and realistic expectations for content and presentational quality of students' work, and high expectations for meeting deadlines.
- Many girls take pride in producing neat work, but obsessively "manicured" assignments can imply a dangerous perfectionism. Encourage risk-taking and trial and error, rather than perfectionism.
- Many girls are comfortable with private reflection but fear public discussion. Class discussion will help them to become more confident about shaping and expressing their ideas.

93 Watch what you say

Words are enormously powerful. What parents and teachers say, and how they say it, can have a much greater impact than most adults realize. I know of one girl who became dangerously thin because her teacher described her as "the fat one," comparing her to her thin sister.

Without realizing it, we can say things that put girls down, humiliate them and damage their self-belief and self-respect. Fathers and father figures are especially prone to engaging in playful, teasing banter with their daughters, using threats, sarcasm and insults as a way of showing love. They may do this partly because straightforward praise and intimacy are strange and uncomfortable to them. However, vulnerable girls will never be certain that no real criticism was meant.

If we want to help our daughters feel loved and cared for, we must try not to make comments or give reprimands that undermine them, even as a joke.

Parents

• Verbal teasing is a form of manipulation that should be used carefully and sparingly.

• Be positive. Give plenty of praise and kind words. These won't make your daughter conceited if you teach that "good at" means "different from," not "better than." We're all good at different things.

• Be aware that when we put our children down, it can be a defense mechanism to protect our own sense of inadequacy.

• Phrases such as, "I can't take you anywhere," "You'll probably end up pregnant," "I don't care what you think," "What's so good about that?" and "You'll never learn" will progressively destroy your daughter's self-esteem and self-belief.

Teachers

• Be positive at all times. Careless and insensitive remarks are taken to heart more than you might imagine or intend.

• Research has shown that confident five-year-olds entering school can become uncertain and develop "learned helplessness" when subjected to constant criticism and negative comments about their work and play.

• It is good for girls to be active as well as to sit quietly. Be sure that your comments don't reinforce submissiveness and discourage more adventurous students from exploring.

94 Loosen the straitjacket

Why are you always so lazy and messy? Why can't you be neat like your sister? She just goes and puts her things away with no arguments. You're just like your father!

"Straitjackets" are statements that lock a person into a role and deny any possibility of change. "You always," "You are just like," "You will never" are typical straitjackets. We all keep developing until the end of our lives. It is unfair in the extreme to hold fixed ideas about anyone, especially a child. Straitjackets can encourage your daughter to become whatever it is you say she is, because she'll give up trying to persuade you that you're mistaken.

Straitjackets come in two forms: 1) labels, insulting and hateful digs that describe what a girl is and what she is not ("You are a moron, an idiot," "You'll never be any good at school," "Why don't you ever finish anything?") and 2) comparisons that unfavorably measure a girl against someone else ("Ginny's much more reliable than you").

Parents

• "Why are you . . . ?" accusations are the most insulting, because they force your daughter to acknowledge your description of her in order to defend herself. "I see you as . . . when . . ." is more acceptable, because it puts the emphasis firmly on your feelings, is specific about the situation and makes clear that she's not always like that.

• Try to move from "Why?" questions to "I" statements.

• Make a mental or written note of the things your daughter "always" does, then be on the lookout to notice when she doesn't conform to the pattern.

• Take the accusations "always" and "never" out of your vocabulary.

Teachers

• Don't compare. When you find yourself teaching children from the same family, never mention the talents or failings of one child to the other.

• Try a class activity in which the students discuss different types of insults and the impact they have: blame, sarcasm and ridicule are forms to consider. Your students can practice using "I" statements instead.

• Unbuckle your own straitjacket. Teachers can be as guilty as parents of failing to revise opinions about individual personalities in the face of evidence to the contrary.

95 Model respect for women

"Mom, why did you let Dad say those things to you and not answer him back? It really upset me to hear it. You must be weak inside."

The best thing a father or father figure can do for the children in his care is to show love and respect for their mother. This reinforces her authority, strengthens the children's respect for her and makes them feel integrated and secure in themselves and in the current family set-up. Most crucial, it also models respect for all women. When girls grow up seeing their mother respected, it helps them to respect themselves and feel good about who they will grow up to be.

If we want to encourage girls to develop a more self-regarding image of femininity, we must model respect for all women, including women teachers and drivers, and the particular strengths and features that women possess. Verbal or physical abuse and violence toward women, and especially to a girl's mother, can be the single most damaging factor to a girl's self-esteem, her mental health and therefore her chances in life.

Parents

- Mothers, don't let your daughters see your sons walking all over you. Children won't grow up learning to respect women if their mothers don't respect themselves. Taking time for yourself and maintaining house rules to protect your interests are marks of self-respect.
- Earn your daughter's respect. If you don't treat others, including her other (possibly absent) parent with due respect, she might question your right to be respected.
- Watch out for the tone and content of your casual remarks when watching movies or television or in the street. Many common insults imply disrespect to women.

Teachers

- Discuss whether you might introduce a sexual harassment policy in your school, if one doesn't exist. Girls should, of course, be prepared to treat boys with the same respect they want to receive in return.
- Gender awareness and equality of respect should apply throughout the school and in every class.

96 Don't swamp her with your success

My dad was a successful self-made man. He did it all on his own and he never let us forget it. He did really well, flashed his money around, and I had no idea how I was going to live up to him, which is what he expected. I was terrified when I left school and the future stared me in the face.

It's surprising how many girls follow in their successful mother's or father's footsteps and do as well, if not better, in the same career. But for every success story, there will be another one, in which the daughter gives up because she feels she can't compete. The danger comes when either parent invests his or her self-worth in a child's success, perceiving this as the only way to gain acceptability. When this happens, the parents are forcing their values and their world onto their daughter, and she may have different plans and interests.

Parents

- Handle your success with sensitivity. Let your daughter see that it results from your interest, commitment and hard work, not your genius—and treat the success as your thing, not something for her to marvel at.
- Be modest. Your success will be evident—being a good role model doesn't mean blowing your own horn.
- Don't try to excel at every activity. Doing something well enough, without comment, and showing that you sometimes fail sets a useful example, too.
- Having two parents who are successful in different fields may make it harder for a girl to find her own niche. This makes it even more important to value the things she likes and does well.

Teachers

- When a student is struggling with something, it won't help her to show how easy it really is by racing through the calculation, explanation or arguments.
- Underachieving students may not feel capable of following in your footsteps, or in those of any other role model. Explain carefully, therefore, each stage on the road to success, to make it appear achievable.

97 What we fear, we bring about

Mom was terrified I'd get into drugs. She never trusted me, checked my things, nosed into where I went and who with, and watched me constantly. I got so fed up that I went out more and got in with a crowd that was, yes, into drugs.

There's a frightening, almost magnetic, force that seems to operate alongside our fears: The more we want something for our daughter, or fear she will or won't do something, the more we seem to sabotage our best intentions. She senses how worried we are and reacts in a negative way. If we're afraid she's going to grow up naughty, we use harsher punishments, which may encourage her to rebel. If we ban candy and cookies from the house, she'll buy them herself and binge when she has the independence and money. If we force her to practice music because she has the talent to excel, she'll lose her love of it and give up.

The common threads in all this are trust and power. If we have little trust, and we use our power inappropriately to manage our fears, we are more likely to turn them into a reality.

Parents

• Identify your fears about your daughter, if any, and ask yourself whether you handle them in a way that may become counterproductive.

• Try to get your fears into perspective. Discuss with someone else how real they are, how important it is that your daughter achieves in the way you wish and, if "the worst" happens, whether it really will be that terrible.

• Cut out the power. Give her as much scope as possible to take care of herself, within your guidelines.

• Reward the behavior you want to see, rather than punishing the lapses, but don't take this to extremes or it will become manipulative.

Teachers

• Identify your fears about a particularly difficult class, or individual or professional relationship. You may be afraid of appearing incompetent, disorganized or too harsh, for example. Reflect on the pattern of your responses and how to change them.

• Think about the fears of the other person or people you have just identified, and how these might interplay with your own.

• Suggest that girls in your class be open about their own fears, in and outside school. They may fear that they are ugly, or appear uncool. Ask how their anxieties color their behavior.

98 The more you use it, the more you lose it

I saw a young boy getting bored while his mother talked with a friend on the sidewalk. He decided to run out toward the road, so his mom grabbed him, dragged him back, hit him and resumed her conversation. He did the same thing again, twice, and so did she. The third time, he ran out into the road, and she hit him harder, several times. The more she hit, the more he chose to disrespect her authority.

There is an important lesson to learn about power, which is that the more you use it, the more you lose it. When power is used or, more accurately, misused frequently, it tends not to stop children doing something but to incite them to further defiance. Perhaps children see adults who have an overreliance on power as weak underneath, and so they exploit this weakness. More likely, they resent the exploitation of their inferior status and skills, and not being understood or treated with the respect they deserve. They then express their frustration with the only power they have—to hit where it hurts.

Parents

• Hitting is not the only power tactic parents use: They also use threats, bribes, harsh punishments and fancy arguments to get their way. Children learn to use these tactics, too.

• We retain authority not by being authoritarian and controlling toward our children, but by continuing to guide, influence, set boundaries for their decisions and, sometimes, direct them if necessary.

Teachers

• A girl who is confident will argue her point if she feels unfairly treated. If you fail to take note and listen to her, you could suffer the consequences later, when she becomes angry and frustrated.

• If you relax your tight control, your authority will not automatically be undermined. Research shows that if you put students more in charge of their own learning, and allow them to evaluate and plan their own and each others' work under your guidance, the number of destructive, power-based challenges declines.

99 Let her grow wings

Independence is a vital and exciting part of growing up for girls. Gaining in competence; experiencing challenges and surviving; experimenting with risks and different ways of doing things; gaining more control over what happens to her; and learning to set her own boundaries are all essential steps a girl must take to become an independent and responsible adult.

Unfortunately, the world outside the home seems to be an increasingly dangerous place. Parents are naturally worried about giving their daughters greater freedom to play and travel without adult supervision. Instead of encouraging their girls to go off on their own and experiment, playing out rope gradually, they tend to supervise, chaperone, constrain and contain them. Children are driven everywhere and discouraged from playing even in the front yard, let alone the street or park. When children are safe indoors, parents can relax. To add virtue to self-interest, they believe that they are doing the best for their child. But managing risk and coping with the unknown increase confidence and are important life and learning skills. Girls need to grow wings and learn to use them.

Parents

• Opportunities to be on her own give your daughter a chance to test herself. Without them, she'll find it harder to establish her identity, develop self-confidence and achieve social adjustment (finding out how to behave in and belong to bigger groups).

• Give her some freedom outside the home gradually, and at first insist that she remain with older siblings or within the safety of a trustworthy group.

• Don't go everywhere by car. Let her travel on the city bus or subway, going with her to begin with, so that she learns her way around in the safety of your company.

Teachers

• Discourage parents from coming to peek at their child through the fence during recess. If she spots them, their daughter could feel spied on and restricted rather than loved.

• Some children learn to use their wings by trying out different ways of working. Treat these trial runs respectfully and be as flexible as possible.

• Classwork in areas such as math or geography can involve the use of local bus and commuter rail schedules, which will enhance self-management skills.

100 Prove your commitment

Inner strength is built on commitment. Children need to feel they have the commitment of at least one significant adult in order to grow up happy, confident, secure and resilient, feeling that they have something to give to others. Birth parents are not the only ones who can offer it. Girls who are able to commit to learning, organizations and friendships despite personal problems usually acknowledge the commitment of someone who spent time with them, showed interest in the things they did, accepted them unconditionally and, most important, was reliable and there in times of need.

Your commitment will enhance your daughter's self-esteem and help her to

- think for herself;
- withstand the pressure of being in a minority of one, yet be flexible enough to compromise on issues of less importance;
- listen to constructive criticism without seeing it as a personal slight; and
- have sufficient curiosity to learn, explore, think and look ahead.

It will ensure that she has the power, and the willpower, to determine and prepare for her future. Her self-confidence, happiness and esteem may depend on your commitment.

Parents

- You can show your commitment to your daughter in many different ways, such as being interested; cherishing her; caring; keeping her safe; offering support; making her birthday special and helping her to make sense of her world.
- She will feel more secure if she knows you think about her when she's not there: "Look, I bought your favorite cookies today!"
- Step-parents and partners have to work harder at commitment, particularly when a girl already feels she's been let down.
- Behaving consistently, such as making and keeping promises to call, write or visit, are essential ways for nonresident parents to show commitment from a distance.

Teachers

- Be aware when a student is going through a tough time. If she loses a parent or close adult through death, separation or illness, she will need a clear commitment from someone like you—even though she may doubt and test it.
- You can show your commitment through patience, tolerance and problem-solving with her when she becomes an adolescent and is not as compliant as she was.
- Never give up on a student. She may give up on herself, but it is your professional and personal responsibility to continue to offer her hope and belief in herself.

Further Reading . . .

Adams, J. *GirlPower: How Far Does It Go?* (Sheffield Centre for HIV and Sexual Health, 1997)

Declaire, Joan, et al. *Raising an Emotionally Intelligent Child* (Fireside, 1998)

Greenspan, Stanley I., M.D., and Jaqueline Salmon. *Playground Politics: Understanding the Emotional Life of the School-Age Child* (Perseus Publishing, 1994)

Hartley-Brewer, E. *Raising Confident Boys: 100 Tips for Parents and Teachers* (Fisher Books, 2001)

Kurcinka, Mary Sheedy. *Kids, Parents, and Power Struggles: Winning for a Lifetime* (HarperCollins, 2000)

Nagy, Allen, et al. *How to Raise Your Child's Emotional Intelligence: 101 Ways to Bring Out the Best in Your Children and Yourself* (Heartfelt Publications, 1999)

Natenshon, Abigail H. *When Your Child Has an Eating Disorder: A Step-by-Step Workbook for Parents and Other Caregivers* (Jossey-Bass, 1999)

Newmark, Gerald, Ph.D. *How to Raise Emotionally Healthy Children: Meeting the Five Critical Needs of Children . . . And Parents Too!* (Newmark Management Institute, 1999)

Paul, Henry A. *When Kids Are Mad, Not Bad: A Guide to Recognizing and Handling Your Child's Anger* (Berkley Publishing Group, 1999)

Pipher, M. *Reviving Ophelia* (Ballantine, 1995)

Seligman, Martin E. P., et al. *The Optimistic Child* (HarperPerennial Library, 1996)

Shapiro, Lawrence E. *How to Raise a Child with a High EQ: A Parent's Guide to Emotional Intelligence* (HarperCollins, 1998)